LIV'S ALONE

LIV'S ALONE

Liv Thorne

HODDER &
STOUGHTON

First published in Great Britain in 2021 by Hodder & Stoughton
An Hachette UK company

This paperback edition published in 2022

1

A CIP catalogue record for this title is available from the British Library

Paperback ISBN 9781529344219
eBook ISBN 9781529344196

Typeset in Celeste by Manipal Technologies Limited

Printed and bound in Great Britain by Clays Ltd, Elcograf S.p.A.

Hodder & Stoughton policy is to use papers that are natural, renewable
and recyclable products and made from wood grown in sustainable forests.
The logging and manufacturing processes are expected to conform
to the environmental regulations of the country of origin.

Hodder & Stoughton Ltd
Carmelite House
50 Victoria Embankment
London EC4Y 0DZ

www.hodder.co.uk

For Herb,
It's all for you.
Mum
x

Liv Thorne is a director of a web design agency, mum to her son Herb, butler to Elvis the 12-year-old terrier and creator of the popular Instagram account @livsalone. Liv is in her early forties, but if you mention that she may flick you. There is a saying that 'everyone has a book in them', she just didn't realise hers would be about buying sperm! Liv, Herb and Elvis can usually be found walking through the fields of Oxfordshire.

CONTENTS

INTRODUCTION

I'm not going to lie, I didn't ever dream it would be like this. As a girl, in my naive fantasies about my life as an adult, not once did I think about having to buy sperm or make the decision to have a baby on my own. I had dreamt of giddy first dates that I'd excitedly tell my friends about because I couldn't keep my hysteria contained for one more second. Dates that would develop into romantic city breaks, sharing plates of antipasti bulging with local delicacies. City breaks that would lead to tightening our belts to pay for our first home together – a real doer-upper with a garden for Basil, our cockapoo. Bricks and mortar that would be the setting for an out-of-this-world proposal that culminated in me wearing an heirloom ring from his great-grandmother because his parents were so smitten with me that they were thrilled to see the glint of their history on my finger. This would be followed by elated tears from my mum to see her baby so very happy, as she immediately set about planning her mother-of-the-bride outfit and dictating who should be on the invite list before a date had even been set. A country wedding would follow, of course, with me practically skipping down the aisle, squeezing my dad's proud hand, followed by Converse-wearing flower girls, before indulging in a lip-smacking feast, drunken toasts and questionable dancing to Whitney. The big day over, my husband and I would jet off to a honeymoon in Iceland (gifted by the in-laws, naturally), which would be documented with unintentional smugness on our social media. Then, twelve weeks later, this perfect life would be superseded by the posting of a blurry black-and-white baby scan and the happy couple beaming with Cheshire-cat smiles.

Sure, some of that has been embellished over the years, and thankfully for my pride, social media didn't exist in the booze-fuelled nineties, but the fact remains that no matter how many times I rewrote my life script, the main elements of it were always the same. There would be a loving relationship, followed by various thrilling chapters with nail-biting twists and turns, which would end with me announcing to my parents that they were to become Granny and Grandad – or Sir, as my dad declared he wanted to be known. Not even in the footnotes of the script had I considered having to buy sperm in order to get pregnant. Fast-forward to 2016, and here I was, aged thirty-seven, fairytale smashed to smithereens, scouring the internet for ways to become pregnant alone.

According to the Human Fertilisation and Embryology Authority (HFEA), the use of donor sperm and donor eggs is on the increase year on year, yet it still only accounts for 3 per cent of those seeking fertility treatment in the UK. As I stood looking at my solo life, I decided that I was going to become part of that 3 per cent. I was going to become a mum using donor sperm, come what may, because without a partner by my side this was the only way I felt I could have a baby of my own. The only thing I knew for certain about what lay ahead was that there was no way I was the only woman in my position – there was a reason why the Bridget Jones sagas hit such a nerve with thirty-something women everywhere, and it wasn't just the big pants. The gentle tick-tock, tick-tock of your fertility in your twenties turns into a fully-fledged cuckoo clock by the time you are thirty-five, a constant screaming reminder that your baby-making time is nearly up. So, with the *Countdown* jingle ever present in my head, having decided I was going to go it alone, I wanted to share my decision and my adventures via a blog, as a story for my future offspring about their conception and also as a reassuring voice to anyone else who was in the same leaking boat.

Well, that was my intention. As it happens, I wrote just five or six blog posts back in 2016, and then I dived headfirst into Instagram as @livsalone, where I quickly felt part of a community and less like I was talking to an empty room – as I had sometimes felt while writing on my blog. On Instagram I shared everything – from smashing the whimsical life plan that we're fed from a young age that having children must follow a wedding, my grief at not getting the life I had thought I was going to have, to buying sperm from Denmark, destigmatising the taboo that is solo parenting and bringing a beautiful baby boy into the world. I discussed the highs and lows of it all. My story piqued the interest of more and more people and I knew that I was beginning to achieve exactly what I had set out to do: to show that while it might not be the 'conventional' way of becoming a mum, that that didn't matter. What mattered was that it *could* be done and this unconventional route should be celebrated. Let's face it, once you become a mum, solo or otherwise, your kid's shit would stink just like everyone else's.

Over the last three years, I have had literally thousands of messages from women who were feeling how I did four years ago – desperate, scared and alone. They have told me that my story has given them courage to believe that motherhood could still be a possibility for them, just when they were beginning to give up hope. One person even let me know I had confirmed to them that they absolutely didn't want to have kids, that it was societal pressure she was feeling rather than the primal ache I had spoken of. Just this week, two people have sent me their positive pregnancy-test photos via Instagram, women I have never met, but who want to share their happiness with me, as I am likely to be the only person they know who can wholeheartedly understand every emotion they are feeling.

It is utterly amazing to me that posting a few home truths online has allowed women who have been struggling to find the words to have honest conversations with their friends about how they are feeling, to genuinely open up. I am told all the time that people have given my details to their friends by way of shining a torch on what could be their future. While I am by no means an authority, I have lived this experience, and the community that has grown over the years has given me as much support in my darkest hours, if not more, than I have ever given to it.

So, this book is the tale of why that thirty-seven-year-old girl added sperm to her shopping list in order to start a family of her own, and all that followed once that momentous decision had been made. Maybe it will shed some light on the first tentative steps of the fertility journey once the 'hilarious' jokes in your late twenties about turkey basting are no longer quite so funny because you have become the punchline, and once the deep primal longing to become a mother is suddenly laid bare, legs akimbo, in a sterile fertility clinic. How does it feel to be the only person walking into NCT classes alone? What on earth do all the fertility acronyms mean?

I can't tell you if becoming a solo mother by choice is something that would work for you – that is not my right, nor what I want to do. However, if you have ever felt that the deafening cries of mainstream media, your parents or your blissfully happy friends telling you 'YOUR EGGS ARE IMPLODING LIKE POP-CORN!' are all becoming too much, this book may feel like a friendly hug to let you know you aren't alone.

So whether you think solo parenthood is the next step for you, or you want to find out how to support a friend who is about to go it alone, or perhaps you just want to know how the hell one person deals with the whirlwind of toddler tantrums because you and your partner are finding it hard enough, then perhaps this book can show you that it really is possible to complete the jigsaw puzzle of life, even if all the corner pieces are missing.

This is my tale – a truthful tale, declaring that 2.4 doesn't have to be the answer to life, the universe and everything.

CHAPTER 1:
THE TIME IS NOW

I was sitting, legs crossed, in the middle of the garden with my back to a large group of friends. The usual clatter of noise that comes from a summer barbecue filled every inch of the air around us – drinks being poured, cutlery scraped, infectious laughter, hyped children and the chitter-chatter of adults excitedly catching up. My friend's daughter ran past me with a kite that was merrily dancing through the sky, and there were at least three children on the squeaking trampoline to my right and one hiding from his sister in the Wendy house, even though she was unaware of the game. The vast garden was literally a hive of cheery activity, yet I was sat in the middle of it, silently sobbing. My eighteen-month-old godson was on my lap, oblivious to the fact that my face was leaking, and his mum was beside me, brimming with concern. She knew why I was crying without me saying a word: I wanted a baby. I desperately wanted a baby.

My maternal instinct didn't jump into my life unexpectedly in my thirties. No, it had been successfully bubbling away since I was a child myself. I became an auntie at the age of thirteen and from that moment on I knew, really knew, that I wanted kids of my own. My university yearbook had me down as the 'Person most likely to . . . turn into Pippa Ross from *Home & Away*'. You may not be au fait with the characters from Antipodean soaps in the nineties, so let's just say that Pippa Ross was the matriarch of Summer Bay. Any waif and stray who so much as dipped a toe into the coastline of that fictional town would end up being adopted by Pippa. Her house was overflowing with drama and love in equal measure. I had been thrilled to be thought of in such high esteem!

Yet, I was single. Well and truly single. The sort of single that doesn't even get a 'plus one' on a wedding invite anymore, nor had done for around a decade; it was deemed futile by the bride and groom because they knew I'd come alone anyway. I had spoken to my friends about looking into sperm donation on many a boozy get-together, yet I always found excuses for why I hadn't taken it any further. I would say it was financial when actually it was due to fear and grief; I was grieving the life that I had always believed would be mine – an exciting life filled with love, a partner and children. Here I was, aged thirty-seven, and there wasn't even a whiff of a shit Tinder date on the romantic horizon. At that moment, as I sobbed while clutching her baby, my friend knew that I had to take my parental destiny into my own hands, and with just one very knowing look and clasp of my hand, she was, without saying a word, gently and reassuringly pushing me towards the cliff edge, encouraging me to leap into the unknown despite the invisible bungee rope of my angst that was always pulling me back – rather like *Thelma & Louise*, but with a less tragic ending!

How the bloody hell did I get here? How on earth had my childhood dreams of introducing my parents to the love of my life, going on to become a blushing bride, followed by the flush of pregnancy and a big house in the country crammed with children, turned into me living all of my adult life alone and ordering sperm online as easily as if it were a leopard-print scarf? Well, getting here was quite the rollercoaster, a real big dipper, one that takes you crashing down just as quickly as it launches you to dramatic heights, and once it is over you are thrilled you decided to get on it in the first place.

Getting to this point had started thirty-seven years ago in Buckinghamshire. I was born the youngest of four in the late seventies. There are fifteen years between me, the youngest, and my brother Mike, the eldest, with my two sisters Sal and Annie, sandwiched in the middle, so our house was always busy with the varied commotion that comes with childhood of all ages – from blaring Howard Jones, tinkering with motorbikes, all the way down to me playing with my plastic Fisher-Price record player. My parents were immensely sociable and the phone literally never stopped ringing. I always remember the screams of 'I'LLLLLL GET IT!' as someone sped down the stairs to the dedicated phone table with its notebook and pen always poised and ready for writing down messages. More often than not it was ringing for Mum, who would sit next to the little table in our hall opposite the rarely used piano, her red nails clasped around the cream receiver as she made arrangements to see her friends. This very often culminated in some sort of dinner party, where the children of the pack would patiently wait for the grown-ups to leave the table so we could knock back any booze left in the plentiful array of glasses scattered about the freshly stained tablecloth that had been starched just hours before. Or we would hit the jackpot by finding an undiscovered After Eight camouflaged by its black paper housing. Like any child of the eighties worth their salt, you could also often find us in the back of my dad's Scirocco in one of a number of pub car parks, overjoyed with the bounty of glass bottles of Coke and packets of prawn cocktail crisps that had been passed through the window by my dad to keep us entertained while he and Mum enjoyed a night out with friends sitting at the bar inside.

My childhood was a really happy one; I have wonderful memories of huge Christmases with big tins of Quality Street and perfectly decorated trees. Of Easter treasure hunts that took five or six cars of all our friends around the county, with the final clue always taking us to a pub before we exchanged Easter eggs. Of playing in my treehouse that Dad had built for me (to be fair, 'treehouse' is quite a grand term for a sheet of MDF wedged between some branches to create a platform, but I didn't care because my dad had built it for me and I loved it). Of amazing holidays in the sun where all I wanted to do was eat chicken and chips and laugh at my friend Emily making a bikini out of coconut shells on the beach. Of having picnics from the back of our car boot at the point-to-point horse race. Of great hugs from my grandparents who lived in the neighbouring village and whom Mum had somehow managed to convince to come to our house every Friday so my two grannies could do the cleaning while my grandad would do some gardening with half a Lambert & Butler hanging from his lips. There was always something happening, never a dull or quiet moment. Like I said, my childhood was a really happy one. Until it wasn't.

I knew something had changed. The whispers around the house were getting more intense and the sobs were getting louder. Mum gently held my hand as I sat on her bed looking out of the small window to the garden. I was eight years old and I remember feeling really uncomfortable with how often she was using the word 'boob' as she told me that she had breast cancer. I have no idea if I knew what that meant, if it was explained to me with brutal honesty or with the gentle tact you use when you discuss with children things that they should never have to understand. I started to stay with friends for long periods, not realising that I was actually being shielded from what was happening at home. Mum didn't ever lose her hair or look any different through my rose-tinted eight-, nine-, then ten-year-old eyes, she was always as seriously glamorous as she had ever been, painted nails, with full make-up on and fashionable clothes. Even visiting her in hospital after she had various treatments didn't unnerve me. In fact, to this day, being in a hospital makes me feel really at ease, I love them. Which, let's face it, is a bloody good job, as I have so often relied on the reassurance within those disinfected walls throughout my pregnancy.

I was taking Mum's illness in my stride. I am sure this is because I really had little clue of the gravity of what was actually happening, and also because I was at a school that I absolutely adored. Truth be told, what was happening at home wasn't my main priority, I just longed to go to school and play Koosh ball with my friends. That is not to say school didn't come with the same playground drama for me as everyone else, though. Like when 'my boyfriend' responded to a letter I had written him in the Easter holidays, in which I had told him I was getting fitted for a bridesmaid's dress for my sister's wedding and he simply replied to me by writing over my letter in a childish scrawl in red ink, 'bet the fitter had a hell of a job' and returning the letter to me. Not before closing the envelope with 'S.W.A.L.F. – Sealed with A Loving Fart.' Hysterical now, but absolutely crushing at the time. I remember insignificant incidents like this with so much more clarity than how I was feeling about the enormity of the fact that my mum was dying, because I had no real concept of what was on the horizon. I did not know what life without cancer was like at that age, so everything felt very ordinary.

To me, life was carrying on much as normal, because that is exactly what my parents wanted me to feel. Every Saturday Dad would still make me go to piano lessons. I hated them so much and was entirely useless, but Dad was adamant he was going to have a musician in the family and, as his youngest, I was very much his last hope. The very silver lining of these weekly piano lessons was that when Dad picked me up, we would go to the local Italian deli, in his car that always smelt of brand-new leather, to get exotic treats for lunch. I loved these trips so much; rare moments of just him and me together. I would constantly fidget with the enormous eighties car phone, which would drive him wild with irritation. In truth, I didn't care too much for this modern technology, I was just trying to keep my hands busy in a desperate bid not to rip open the paper packaging housing the salty salami that sat on my lap and snaffle every last morsel before having to share it with everyone else when we got home. Dad would ignore my restlessness by singing along to Meatloaf as if his very existence depended on it.

I don't ever look back and feel like regular life had been halted, as if I was missing out because of Mum's illness. Quite the opposite – reliving those years makes me feel exhausted with how much we crammed in. With the benefit of hindsight, I really believe this was partly due to the fact that my parents shielded me so well and also that life as they knew it was constantly flashing before their eyes. The Easter treasure hunts were soon to be one passenger less, the chink of glasses on the Spanish veranda would be a note lower, with one person missing from the family photo, Father Christmas was to be a man once more and my grandparents were going to have to kiss their daughter goodbye forever. Mum was no longer going to be the skipper of the boat leading me to calm waters after teenage heartbreak.

Yet, no matter what landscape we thought we were going to have to navigate without Mum, nothing could have prepared us for the fact that, despite her cancer diagnosis, it wasn't Mum who died prematurely, but Dad. Through my hazy memory I remember that at some point, not too long after Mum got the initial all-clear, Dad, an uber-fit and healthy man, started to feel his body change. He knew something was wrong.

It may have been that it was a stifling hot day when I was told, at eleven years old, that Dad had asbestos poisoning, or it was just a long, hot, uncomfortable summer, but I just know that whenever I think of that time, I feel too hot. The type of heat that makes you feel itchy, that there is nowhere to hide, no shade, no escape. In stark contrast to Mum's previous illnesses, the decline in Dad was obvious and rapid. His rugby player, marathon-runner body was constantly changing shape, becoming weaker and thinner, while his handsome face gained the gleaming puffiness that comes with steroid medication. The asbestos he had used to insulate a barn on the family farm thirty years before had mutated into a disease that was ravaging every single part of his body. Despite the initial prognosis being that he had just three months to live, Dad managed to survive the aggressive torment for eleven months. Those months gave us all time to say good-bye, allowed him to walk my eldest sister down the aisle, enjoy crabbing on the Cornish coast once more and take me to our Italian deli just a handful more times.

Dad died, aged forty-nine, when I was twelve years old. I was on a week-long school trip on the south coast and remember being asked to go to the office of the youth hostel, where I was told on the phone that he had died. I have absolutely no idea who it was on the other end of the line that broke that news to me. I do remember, though, being told that my best friend's parents were to collect me and drive me back home, so that I could say goodbye to him before his body was taken from our living room where he had spent his final weeks dramatically demanding cornflakes. It was the longest car journey; I remember feeling so far away from everything that felt normal, and as if the motorway beneath us was never going to end, that we would be on it forever, going faster and faster and yet never getting home.

Obviously, I did get home, I got to say goodbye and I got to feel my mum's arms around me in a grip that I had never felt before.

Dad's funeral was vast; it was a bright sunny day filled with laughter and bittersweet storytelling in a marquee in the garden at our family home. We ate a giant pork pie, as his food distribution company had started out making pork pies and quiche, and anyway, who wants quiche Lorraine at a funeral when you can have a giant pork pie with your name emblazoned on it? His gravestone reads, 'He had a go' and I can assure you he most certainly did.

Dad's death was the start of me ensuring my mind never remembered anything I thought would cause me pain – like who it was that told me he had died. The immediate aftermath is not something I can remember at all, as I didn't allow my mind to register it. I know I went back to school pretty quickly after, which would have been my choice, and my boyfriend dumped me as soon as we saw each other on my first day back. I was brimming with excitement to see him, believing the news of my dad's death may even make him give me a hug (the peak of childhood affection!). What I hadn't expected, though, was for him to tell me that he wanted to dump me on the school trip but hadn't got round to it. I was twelve years old, so obviously we weren't in an actual relationship, and I am not sure we had even held hands, yet I remember my insides doing cartwheels when I saw his beaming face in the school corridors. So for him not to feel the same, crushed all my pre-teenage romantic hopes. I suspect I poured my grief into the sadness I felt about being dumped, because that was far easier to explain to myself than the fact that I was never going to see my dad again.

Soon after Dad died, Mum and I left the sprawling Buckinghamshire countryside for a beautiful town-house in Oxford with a tiny courtyard garden. I was constantly trying to find the happiness I had had at my primary school, so I went to three schools in less than two years, hopelessly seeking somewhere I felt content. My poor mum was desperate to do anything she could to ensure I was happy, and I knew it. As a typically selfish teenager, what had never dawned on me was the fact that Mum was maybe dealing with her own demons too. Less than two years after Dad died, Mum had to tell me that her cancer had returned. She had secondary breast cancer, the ultimate prize for the Grim Reaper.

Again, life shifted, and we knew what was coming as we had literally just watched it happen to Dad. My worries were all rooted around me, like the A-grade self-absorbed teenager that I was. Who would walk *me* down the aisle? Where would *I* live? Who would pay for *my* holidays? Who would hold *my* hand when my heart was broken? I cannot even imagine how this time was for Mum; she had already watched her husband of twenty-seven years have to say goodbye to their children and now she was going to have to prepare for the same shitty fate. I am not sure what would have been worse – the mental or the physical pain she had to endure over the next couple of years. There was nothing we could do to ease her pain, and time and life ploughed on regardless.

I went to an all-girls school in Oxford, which offered me little to no support for what was happening at home. I was often branded a troublemaker and singled out as an example of bad behaviour when all I wanted was a teacher to ask if I was OK, if I was really OK, and if they could offer me any help. But nobody did. My mum was paying through the nose for my education, primarily in order for me to get some additional support and space away from the fact she was at home dying and that I had lost Dad so recently. However, the support I was offered was nothing short of comical in the fact that there was none. Back in the mid-nineties, mental health wasn't so openly discussed as it is now, so how I was coping wasn't on their pastoral radar. I don't know where the circle started or ended but the school treated me badly and I treated them badly in return, by permanently being what they often described in my reports as 'spirited'.

Mum and I lived next to one of the busiest pubs in Oxford, and from the age of fourteen my best friend Jen and I would drink in there every Friday and Saturday night. We had elaborate stories ready should anyone ask us what we did, to ensure our cover was never blown and they would not realise we were wildly underage. I would tell people I was a radio DJ in the evenings on Mix96 in Aylesbury, which is why I could never go out during the week, and Jen would say that she was doing an art foundation course at Oxford Brookes. I had done a short work experience stint at Mix96, so I had some background knowledge should anyone ask me any questions. Honestly, sometimes we were so convincing even I believed us! The arrogance of my youth never once allowed me to think that I would be caught. I had been drinking there so long that on my sixteenth birthday they held a 'twenty-first' birthday party for me. I mean, they must have known I wasn't twenty-one, but no one let on. Two years later I came clean about my age because I was coming up to eighteen and I wanted to start working there, which I knew meant I would have to hand over some official documents that would blow my cover. Everyone pretended to be shocked, yet I am sure they were just as relieved as I was that the weak stories about my DJing life could stop. So a couple of weeks later, they held an official eighteenth birthday celebration for me and I started work there the very next week.

Those nights in the cellar bar of that pub in the mid-nineties, with Jen by my side, were some of my very happiest memories, despite the turmoil of what was happening at home, just metres away. Our house was so close that I would take one of the handsets of our home phone with me to the pub, and if Mum wanted or needed me to come back, she would press the button that you use to find the phone when you lost it down the back of the sofa. It would beep and beep and beep in my handbag until I realised and rushed home. The pre-iPhone mobile phone! I am sure she allowed me this kind of freedom because she knew I was happy and seeing me happy would have meant the world to her. Also, I didn't get in trouble with the police, didn't take drugs or bring boys home, I would just go to the pub next door and drink as much Mad Dog 20/20 as it was possible to do in three hours and chain-smoke Marlboro Reds. It was my way of relieving all the tension at school and my fear of losing my mum to cancer in the not-too-distant future.

At one point, during my GCSE year, Mum went on holiday with her boyfriend (who I of course hated at the time but have since realised is a gem of a man), and I saw that as the opportunity of a lifetime to take the week off school. I told my teachers that Mum was in the hospice and that I was going to go and spend some quality time with her. Instead, I went home and set about telling everyone at the pub that I was having a week off my relentless DJ schedule and I spent the days mixed between having pints and stuffed potato wedges at the pub and Ribena and stale sandwiches at home. I was having the time of my fifteen-year-old life. That was until the house phone rang and I stupidly answered it – it was my brother. At fifteen years older than me he was always the one person who could strike fear into my very core! The call went something along the lines of:

'Why are you at home?'

'Oh, I was just nipping back to get a book.'

'Liv, I am sat with Mrs Barbour in her office, they have not seen you all week.'

Oh. Shit. Well and truly rumbled.

I am sure my punishment was bad, although I have no idea what it was. I was the living embodiment of being given an inch and taking a mile. I was getting away with murder.

I didn't help with Mum's care at all, in fact, I actively avoided it, just getting by with minimal offerings like putting her tablets that had already been dosed out on her bedside table ready for her to swallow. Or, if I was feeling really kind, I would help her up to the loo. That was the extent of it. I would rather spend my time escaping home life by being at the pub or spending hours and hours trawling through the CDs in HMV, while everyone else had to deal with the complexities of Mum's care. Much like my early childhood, I don't have particularly harrowing memories of that time in my life. I had become a true master of convincing everyone I was doing just fine, thank you very much. I recently asked my sisters if I was ever given or offered counselling. Of course I had been. I had had counselling at Mum's brilliant hospice, yet I convinced the doctors that I was absolutely fine. Nothing to see here. Move along please. And I have been doing that, with Oscar-worthy ability, ever since.

Mum had a lot of fun in the few years leading up to her death. Dad had left some money and she knew she was going to die, so she made sure she enjoyed every second of the time she had left. We had six-week-long summer holidays with the whole family, including the grandchildren that had now joined our clan. She took me to Harvey Nichols so that the incredible M.A.C make-up artists, who had just reached our shores, could teach me how to apply my make-up. She went on girls' trips to New York, bringing me back a bottle of the perfume that I still wear to this day. She hired Chewton Glen for her fiftieth birthday celebrations, where we all, including my beauty-treatment-averse brother, had various spa treatments so that we were on sparkling form for the big blow out. She knew how to have fun and she squeezed out every last bit that she could until her body just couldn't take it anymore.

I was on holiday with my godparents in Spain when I was told that Mum was very ill and being flown back to the UK from her holiday, also in Spain. We had had this sort of scare before, but this one felt different. All the emotions I had when I was away from home and told that Dad had died came flooding back. I just wanted to be back in Oxford – I needed to be with my brother and sisters and to hold Mum. I didn't want to go out and drink Malibu and Coke and unsuccessfully flirt with boys at Discoteca He-Ho anymore. I suddenly decided, having shunned any involvement for so long, that I wanted to be part of the discussions at home about what was going to happen next. I didn't leave Spain early, though, it wasn't deemed necessary, and I got home, as scheduled, a few days later, desperate to hold her. We all got to spend time with Mum, reminisce, brush her hair and say our goodbyes, but eventually there was just no stopping the cancer that was clawing at every organ and bone in her body. She died peacefully aged just fifty, when I was seventeen years old, knowing that she was so very loved. I had just managed to tell her that I had got a U in the one A level I had taken that year. She must have been so proud!

Immediately after Mum died, we all went to her favourite restaurant, which opened early for us so that we could celebrate the way she would have wanted us to: with food and booze. We were shell-shocked, but I remember very clearly the feeling of relief that she didn't have to go through all that anymore. That she was no longer in pain and neither were we, as we were no longer waiting for the inevitable outcome. We stayed at that table in that light-filled restaurant with the huge lemon tree in the middle for what felt like hours, surrounded by the thick debris of our mournful consumption. I am the master of eating my feelings and that day was no different. We shed tears, we told stories, we laughed, we hugged, we celebrated our darling mum. My brother, now the head of our household aged just thirty-two, picked up the bill. He has been picking up the bill for us ever since.

The next year or so was a huge blur – like a sped-up film montage, where I can remember certain things that happened but not with clarity and not in a cohesive timeline. While Mum was alive, one of the many conversations we had had about The Future was where I was going to live when she was gone. Somehow, offers from my siblings and godparents were pushed aside and Mum and I had decided together that I was going to live with some family friends. They weren't in my parents' inner circle and we saw that as a really good thing, like a new beginning rather than trying to cling on to the past. They had sons a little younger than me, so their house was already full of hormones and it seemed that lil' ol' me joining their gang wouldn't mean the end to anyone's retirement or anything, just an additional bum on the sofa. The real clincher was that they had dinner together every day, as a family. Mum and I loved the thought of this as it was something that we had struggled to do, what with her often being bed-bound and me very busy pretending to be a local radio DJ and failing my exams.

When we sold the house Mum and I lived in, I moved back to the countryside with my New Family. Their house was being renovated and I remember it feeling very chaotic, very busy, very not like home. We were all trying too hard, yet simultaneously not hard enough. I learnt to drive so I could come and go with freedom, yet still I felt so detached from what my life had been just months before. I could hardly neck pints of Kronenbourg with all my friends at the pub before hopping into my Peugeot 106 and driving back to my new house forty minutes away. There was literally nothing that felt the same. I had no anchor. Except for my brilliant array of eclectic friends at college . . .

I ended up studying for my A levels at a sixth form college mainly for those retaking their exams, students from outside the UK hoping to have a better chance of being accepted into a British university if they gained a British qualification, and for education fuck-ups like me. There was the most amazingly diverse crew there – from Spanish royalty to American athletes. Coming from my all-girls boarding school a mile down the road, this was like having all my senses stimulated at the same time.

I had been completely besotted with one of my friends for quite some time and we finally got together fairly soon after Mum had died. He had known Mum and was truly sad when he found out she had died that summer. He used to call her the Dog's Bollocks because he thought she was so cool. It was maybe not the elegant nickname she would have hoped for, but I know she would have bloody loved a hot Spanish boy thinking she was a winner. It was so important to me that he knew her, as I had realised the chances were that only a very few people in my future would have known how incredible my mum was, so those that did I wanted to keep close.

He and I had a very messy, naive, funny, drunken, mistake-riddled relationship. I absolutely doted on him; I knew he was really fond of me, but to be honest he smoked so much weed he would have been numb to anything too deep. After college we knew we were to go our separate ways – if not different countries, then very definitely different universities – so despite me wanting so badly to cling on to those sloppy and chaotic months, I knew they were coming to an end. He wrote me a goodbye letter so beautiful that it still makes me cry when I read it. I cried even more when I found out about ten years later it was actually his best friend who had fired up the huge computer in their grubby shared house and written those words on his behalf! Our break-up also coincided with me leaving my New Family. I felt like I was letting Mum down and I hated the thought that she wouldn't know where I was anymore, but for one reason or another, things were just not working out and I didn't have the energy to pretend they were anymore.

So, at just eighteen years old, I was orphaned, single and while not exactly homeless, I didn't have my own home. I moved in with my sister closest in age to me, Annie, and her husband, who had recently got married so that we could make sure Mum got to be mother of the bride one final time. They were both just twenty-four and suddenly had what was essentially an un-housetrained eighteen-year-old daughter. They lived in Oxford and I was so thrilled to be back. While I felt a sense of security when the dreaming spires were looming over my every move, I also thought I should go to university. That is just what happened in Middle England: you got your A levels, you went to university and then you moved to London, with little thought of how privileged your gilded life was. No Gap Yah for me, though, there was no way I wanted to put myself a plane ride away from my family – I wanted to be as close as possible to them after everything that had happened.

The problem with assuming I should go to university, however, back when it was a free privilege, is that I had monumentally fucked up my exams. Actually, it wasn't the exams as much as the very fact I had completed little to no work throughout sixth form at all, and the exams were just the mouldy cherry on the unsatisfying cake. The only thing I categorically knew was that I wanted to be Chris Evans, as his effervescence, his zest for life, really lured me in. The years of lying about being a radio DJ had almost convinced me that was the life I was going to lead one day. The problem with wanting to be Chris Evans and having one A level to my name was that the only university that would take me was in Warrington. The degree was awarded by the University of Manchester, but everything relating to the degree was based in Warrington. The only things I knew about that place were that it was very, very far away from anything I knew, and also that Chris Evans grew up there. It was a done deal. We trundled up the M6, my ever-supportive sisters and I, in two cars full to the brim with all my stuff. I needed my room in halls to feel like home. We exited the M6 and went around 358 roundabouts until we came to the old army barracks that was to be my new base, where we set about making my room feel less like a prison cell, with fairy lights, my cardboard cut-out of Tintin, photos of Mum and Dad and more CDs than HMV. We giggled and laughed, anticipating how much fun I was going to have over the next three years. Just what I needed. They poured me a large gin and tonic and waved me a teary goodbye. After they shut the door, I continued to polish off most of the bottle of gin to try to muster the courage to talk to the people milling around outside. Having had so much confidence in my 'old life' in Oxford, this was the very moment that I can say I started a lifelong, deep-rooted and complicated relationship with depression and anxiety.

While nothing specifically bad happened to me in Warrington, they were the three most unhappy years of my life, no contest. I made some great friends and I met some really good, funny, kind people, yet nothing felt right as I was so far from my family, from Oxford, from my friends. Not to mention that Mum had died less than a year before and my grief must have been so raw. I have very few regrets in my life but going to university gets the gold prize. It was categorically the wrong thing for me to do at that time. I was very much the outsider, which is not something I had ever experienced before, as I had usually been the one connecting all the dots between groups of friends, never the outlier. Keeping in contact with people at home was hard, too, there was no social media, mobile phones were around but hardly ever used and so everything felt very disparate. In my first year I still had to queue to use the phone under the stairs, the air around it always thick with hot farts and stale cigarettes. I used to cry down the phone to my sisters, explaining how unhappy I was, and yet I wasn't sure what alternative I had but to ride it out. It was not like I could go home to Mum and Dad.

In the holidays I would split my time between my sister's house, which was now in Hackney, and a pub that some friends were managing back in Oxford. They were always happy to have me there, and for the next few years, that pub felt like home, where I was welcomed back from Warrington with excitement and plates of cheesy chips. Inexplicably, I had lost contact with all my friends from school apart from a couple, so when I was back in Oxford, I literally spent my whole time at the pub. Therefore it seemed sensible that when that long, hard, lonely stint up north finally finished and my 2:2 in radio production (no joke) was added to my list of incredible academic achievements, I should move into the pub.

The next few years were the polar opposite of my uni days. I felt settled, I had a big group of friends, I got a job in London and continued to spend my days moving between Hackney and Oxford. Even the four-hour round-trip commute on the bus to and from London each day didn't dampen how thrilled I was to no longer be at university. Of course, the reason I didn't fully commit to London was because of a boy. Well, a man actually; he was maybe eight or nine years older than me but definitely a boy in attitude. He had long hair, an infectious laugh, a VW camper and I adored him. Though the very fact I didn't even have his phone number should tell you everything about how serious our relationship was. I would give anything to be able to show twenty-one-year-old me all the red flags that gave away how little he thought about our relationship, in stark contrast to how important I felt it was. Like the time he announced to our friends one Friday night around the pub table that he was only with me for my beautiful face, certainly not my body. He wasn't a bad or vicious person, quite the opposite, but he definitely wasn't kind to me, although I know this wasn't deliberate, just naive. It culminated in him forgetting to tell me we were no longer an item. We had absolutely nothing in common and we were the world's most unlikely couple; however, it would have been handy had he have let me know that one of us had realised that at last! I happily rocked up to a bar for his brother's birthday party where, a couple of hours later, he left with another girl. Apparently, everyone knew we were no longer together, and they were all shocked I had turned up. I was crushed. Totally crushed and embarrassed. A couple of days later I saw him with his new girlfriend, and it made me feel so utterly desolate that I ran into a car park and threw up. It was also the first and only time that I ever considered harming myself, as I thought about walking in front of a passing bus. Of course, I didn't, and I don't think I even vaguely wanted to really, but I vividly remember staring at that bus and wanting it to make all the pain go away.

I couldn't take any more. No more heartache. No more pain. No more being abandoned. I couldn't have one more person I loved leave me. So, brick by brick, year after year, I built up an invisible emotional wall to protect me from any more pain. It is no surprise to me now that this was the last relationship I was in. Relationship being quite a strong word for it, too, if I'm honest. Don't get me wrong, it is not like I have left a trail of men weeping at my rejection, quite the opposite, in fact, I think I coined the phrase 'friend-zoned'!

Not allowing myself to be in a position where I could get hurt again didn't mean not having fun, though. By my mid-twenties I had bought a house with some money that Mum and Dad had left me and a whacking great big mortgage. I finally had a home, one that was mine, and I was so grateful. I filled it with all my belongings that had been sat in a cold storage unit since Mum died. It felt wonderful, truly wonderful. I had also landed a job in a marketing agency in Oxford which gifted me the most brilliant set of friends. With true dedication to my social life, I bought a house within feet of the local music venue, one of the best bars in town and a butcher. What more could I possibly need? Every week I would go to as many gigs as I could – from watching Adele support Metronomy in front of around fifty people, to a packed-out gig for the Arctic Monkeys – then usually rock up to work the next day, still half-cut, to be taken out for a boozy lunch by the *Sunday Times* to lure us into spending our clients' advertising budget with them.

It was how your twenties should be: hazy, carefree, short days and long, sticky-floored nights. I had learnt to look over my shoulder, though, knowing my life played out like a scene from *Total Wipeout* – running along happily and then – THWACK! – you're knocked down, only to get back up again and be punched in the face by a red-gloved hand that came out of nowhere. The problem with always faking that you are OK and that your emotional wall is protecting you, is that if some turmoil does leak through the cracks and get to you, the whole wall crumbles and you feel exposed again. All three of my grandparents died within three years, the death of my glorious Grandad leaving me with a hole in my heart that will never be filled. My sister and her family moved to France, which felt like such an epic loss to me that it took me a long time to adjust to the fact that she wasn't within Sunday-roast distance and that I wouldn't be able to be as big a part of the lives of her three kids as I had envisaged. Then there were always the highs: the festivals, the road trips, the long pub lunches that turned into messy nights out. On the surface everything was very normal, yet throughout, there was never so much as a whiff of a man. I fell for deeply inappropriate people, knowing, deep down, it would never go anywhere. It is pretty hard to fall in love when you won't even go on a second date for fear of someone finding a chink in your armour and marching right on in and scooping up your fragile heart only for them to break it again.

My being single became a casual joke. It starts with engagement parties, doesn't it? That is the beginning of the barrage of feel-good celebrations that you assume will happen to you one day. Endless years of celebrating other people's happiness. Like well-placed dominoes, the engagement party sets off the hen do, then the wedding, the anniversary, the baby shower, the christening, the first birthday party . . . even bloody divorce parties. Slowly, year after year, you can relate less and less to the daily flotsam and jetsam of the lives of your closest friends. Once you have been single for a long time, you get very good at being single, so the looking for a partner becomes less sincere even if the longing doesn't. You still yearn for what the couples around you have; the supportive touch on the shoulder as you brush past each other, having someone to tell when you are going to be late home from work, someone to have a good argument with, someone else to look at the leak under the sink with you, someone to have midnight chats with about what we would call our children, someone to hold your hand when you are scared. Christ, I would give almost anything just for someone to tell me what to have for dinner every now and again. My friends started getting married quite young, too – as I type this, my best friends are celebrating their twenty-year wedding anniversary. We are the same age, yet they have had the reassurance of someone loving them back for twenty years, while I have not even mustered up twenty dates!

Somewhere in my late twenties, I inexplicably left the job I loved and started working for a company where I essentially worked alone, in a barn, in the middle of a farmyard. I began to withdraw more and more from my friends and my anxiety was through the roof – by which I mean it was crippling. When everyone around you is beginning to live a different life to you, one that you are desperate to be part of, you have to retreat and build the wall higher. It got to the stage where I would leave work on a Friday night and not speak to one other person until Monday morning, often I wouldn't even leave the house. If I had to go to the supermarket, I would have my phone clamped to my ear always chatting aimlessly to my patient sister, so I didn't feel like I was in there alone, filling my trolley with way more than I needed, to make it look like I was buying for my imaginary partner, as if people were checking. I would try to avoid social situations or make sure I was in charge of them, so I could control when they ended or where they were held. Everything just became heavy, there was no lightness. I was the master of a tears of a clown facade; most people would have had no idea that when I was out being the life and soul, it was taking every single ounce of energy or mental capacity that I had. Then on the hangover days,

I would assume my friends would be seeing their parents, or their boyfriend's parents or their grandparents for Sunday lunch and I just had my hangover anxiety for company. I would spend weekends driving round and round Oxford just to pass the time, scouting out family homes I wanted to live in with my non-existent partner and kids. Eventually I ended up buying a dog, a glorious scruffy boy who ensured I had to leave the house every day, into the fresh air. Even though all the comments about him being a baby replacement made my heart hurt with embarrassment and longing, it didn't matter, because that little dog, Elvis, saved me.

He was the one who would be by my side when I would get the dreaded calls . . . the 'I've got something to tell you' calls. I knew what it was, I always knew what it was. They were calling to tell me the brilliant news that they are pregnant. Another baby. By this stage I had ten nieces and nephews and was a godparent to seven children. The calls were just confirmation of one less person to understand my single life as an adult. Anxiety can make your thought processes very selfish; you are genuinely happy for them, yet still you have to muster the enthusiasm of an honest smile, like a loser at the Grammy's. The knot in your stomach becomes tighter as you feel like you are constantly being punched there, and the longing becomes acute. You are carrying around your womb every day like empty Tupperware. Every thirty seconds it feels like you are reminded that you *must be pregnant by thirty-five* or your womb will dry out at that exact second and your ovaries will combust.

Then, suddenly, I am thirty-seven, alone, lonely, being able to count on one hand the number of true single friends I have, being unintentionally omitted more and more from the lives of my friends that, through no fault of their own, revolve around even numbers around the dinner table, hordes of children and school-gate friends. I cannot participate in chat about nursery fees, or how annoying it is that my other half had four nights out this month while I haven't had one. It feels like all I can offer is epic Netflix recommendations, because I have completed all its levels. It is like you start out in a Venn diagram of friendship with a huge common section in the middle, that slowly begins to separate, until it leaves you feeling like there are two entirely separate circles and all you want to do is belly flop with gusto into their circle, but it feels impenetrable due solely to circumstance, not lack of love.

All of this – each little insignificant comment to each monumental trauma – has culminated in me continuing to build up my wall, brick by brick, row by row. It's a real corker of a wall, with barbed wire on every inch yet adorned with fairy lights and disco balls to convince people that everything inside is completely and utterly fine. One that would protect me from ever being hurt again. The wall that has stopped me from ever succumbing to the opportunity of happiness in a relationship. The wall that means my one true longing of becoming a mother was becoming more and more unlikely. I didn't want a baby to put a plaster over my historical pain, I wanted a baby because that is what every cell in my body was telling me it needed. That is what I knew had to happen. That is what my friend knew had to happen at that fateful barbecue. I no longer glorified marriage. I no longer felt that my life had to start and end with being someone's wife. I had to take the leap alone. That was it; I was going to leap right over that bloody wall that I had so carefully built. I was going to go and get spunked!

CHAPTER 2:
ADD SPERM TO
PRAM?

Thinking about getting pregnant and buying sperm to do so suddenly filled every waking minute. I felt so alive. Like I was on the cusp of something truly amazing. Suddenly the nappy adverts on the TV didn't make my soul hurt, they made my whole body tingle with anticipation. I needed to tell people, to make this real. You know when once you have said something out loud you can't really go back? So, I decided I had to tell my family about my decision. Telling them was going to be the litmus test of whether this was something so beyond the realms of possibility that I really should quit before I started. They were the people who knew me inside out, and they were also the people without whose support this really could be nothing more than a pipe dream. I was teetering on the edge of making my dreams come true, but if one of them expressed even the smallest bit of doubt, it would have infected my excitement.

I decided to call Annie first, the one I lived with when Mum died. This was a very strategic decision – she was the family barometer. If there was anything that people wanted to say but they felt awkward bringing it up, Annie would absolutely say it, no hesitation! Not because she is unkind – quite the opposite, she wants everything to work out well, so she covers all angles in terms of possible outcomes. She will always, always think of a scenario that you haven't. So making that call to her was huge. While I was determined to get pregnant with or without my family's support, I knew that having them with me would be the solid foundation I needed and really wanted. I tried to call her three times, leaving messages, sending texts. Each time my adrenaline would rocket and then drop, and I would get slightly breathless.

Finally, I got hold of her. I was sitting in a park in town, under a tree overlooking a massive pond. It was a warm summer day and there were people milling around me everywhere, which made me acutely aware of what I was just about to say. Out loud. In public. I didn't want everyone to hear this. Why on earth had I decided to call her while I was out? I went to put the phone down and call another time. Of course, as soon as I removed the phone from my ear, I heard her voice. 'Hey babe.' I panicked at the sound, so I just blurted out, 'I am going to get pregnant.' There was silence. Probably only a second or two, but it felt like years. Then, finally, an excited 'wow!'. Of course, she had needed time to let that information sink in. It is not every day your terminally single thirty-seven-year-old sister calls you to tell you she is going to have a baby on her own. I mean, who did I think I was, the Virgin Mary? We chatted briefly about how I was going to do it. When I say briefly, I mean briefly, because I literally had no idea other than the fact that I needed to get hold of some sperm somehow. We talked about my health – both mental and physical – about finances, about support, and about all the practical things I knew she would cover. Yet what she didn't say was that she thought I shouldn't or couldn't do it. The relief was huge. I put the phone down, crying, but with a real spring in my step. It was everything I had wanted to hear.

With what felt like the approving pat on my back that I needed from my sister, I then immediately called my eldest sister, Sal. As soon as I told her the plan, she cried and made various proclamations in a voice at least two octaves higher than her usual one. She couldn't have been happier. She knew this was everything I had longed for and she was thrilled I was going to go and make it happen. She too had concerns, but I largely closed my ears to those as they were things out of my control, so I just listened to the sentences of excitement and support. Like when you have just got back from the supermarket run before a party and someone asks if you have enough booze. You don't listen or focus on that part, you just can't wait for the party to start.

Next up, my brother. Let me tell you, men do not like talking about sperm! They are not used to talking about their bodily functions in the same way that women are. So when I started talking to him about my plans, his first reaction was to move away from the topic of *how* I was going to get pregnant and swiftly readjust to much more practical subjects like the cost of fertility treatments. I told him I was going to look into remortgaging my house in order to get enough money together. He sounded genuinely excited, but my brother likes facts and I didn't have any. That, coupled with my overuse of the word 'sperm', meant that with his full unwavering support behind me, our chat was over.

Fuck! That was it, I had ripped the plaster off, there were a few painful hairs attached, but ultimately, it was done. The wild cat had pounced out of the bag. It was official. I had told the people I loved the most about my plan, and now there was no turning back. Thank god. I was going to make this happen.

It is all very well deciding you are going to get pregnant and telling people your maternal plans, but where on earth do you start? It is like knowing you are craving a katsu curry; you think you probably know all the ingredients you need, yet you have no idea how to turn the sum of those parts into the sweet and crispy curry that is making your mouth water. So, you go to where all bad research starts, Google, and you eagerly type in 'katsu curry recipes'. Seconds later, 1,334,853 results pop up, as there is no definitive way to make it. Becoming pregnant alone is similar, yet there are just two ingredients: eggs and sperm. How on earth can marinating just two ingredients come with so very many alternative cooking methods?

The excitement became clouded by a thick blanket of confusion. I am a real bull-in-a-china-shop type of person; once I have made a decision, I need to get on and do it now, now, now before any self-doubt creeps in. So the first thing I did was call my GP to book an appointment.

'Is it urgent?' the kind receptionist asked.

'Not really, I just want to find out how to get pregnant.'

She must have thought it was fairly critical, as I was given an appointment the next day. She maybe thought I just needed a sex ed lesson.

I didn't sleep that night. Not only was it a rare tropical UK day, with an equally sticky evening, but I was a ball of anxiety. What if the doctor laughed at me? What if she asked me a question I didn't know the answer to and put on my records that I was UNFIT TO BE A MOTHER because of it? I felt like I was going to a job interview. I had prepared the answers to the questions I thought I would be asked and for the only time in my life I KNEW the answer to 'where do you want to be in ten years' time?' I wanted to be at my child's sports day. I wanted to be making plans for the school holidays. I wanted the house to be noisy. I wanted to be so tired I felt like I was hallucinating.

I waited with sweaty palms in the huge modern reception of my doctor's surgery, my heart beating so fast I felt lightheaded. A handsome young doctor appeared and called his next patient. (Seriously, he was so young, proper *Doogie Howser, M.D.* territory.) I suddenly felt really old, too old to even start this, surely? Even doctors suddenly seemed *much* younger than me, so imagine how I would feel at the school gates? There was no more time to ponder dramatic scenarios, though, as my full name was bellowed across the room by the affable young receptionist. I walked for what seemed like miles to my doctor's office, tripping over my own feet, suddenly very aware of all my limbs and not knowing where to place any of them, while at the same time trying to count the requisite number of doors to reach my destination, as instructed.

I poked my head around the door as if not quite ready to allow my full body to enter. The doctor had a kind face, thank god. She motioned at me to sit down in the chair next to her, so I obliged and immediately went into full chat mode. I am a chatterer; I get nervous and I chat (unless I am at a party where I don't know anyone, then I become mute and head to the kitchen to be 'helpful'). I warned her that I was going to cry. I cry at adverts, so of course I am going to cry when I am telling the medical equivalent of Father Christmas what is written at the top of my wish list, because I have been a good girl this year. On cue I burst into tears. I told her that there was nothing wrong, that on the contrary, I was going to tell her something great.

Spluttering, I eventually blurted out, 'I want a baby, I need sperm!' Thankfully, she laughed – not in an unkind way, I think she was just relieved I didn't say something more sinister. She didn't send me to the Naughty Step to think about what I had said. She said, 'Of course you do, you are thirty-seven, let's get on with it.' I must have visibly relaxed in the overly waxed seat (my nails had managed to dig half a centimetre down in the previous minute). I felt like she had just approved me. Like the notion of me becoming a mum wasn't the most ridiculous thing she had ever heard. She even seemed excited. We talked about my weight (I have been overweight since I was about six, when diet yoghurts started to hit the shelves and Rosemary Conley was telling everyone their hips and bums were too big. My mum, a size eight, lapped up the new diet culture and took me with her, which, in turn, started a really unhealthy relationship between me and food that I haven't addressed as I should). The doctor told me about a diet she'd heard of that excluded eating any vegetables for two weeks. I politely declined and said I would look into alternatives. She told me that every half stone I lost, the better my chances were. I knew this. I know this. I would be on it! I should have been on it before. I know.

'You know solo parenthood is going to be hard, really hard?' she asked me.

'Yes, yes I know. I have been surrounded by children since I was thirteen. I know that everything is going to change. Everything. I'm ready.'

'You know it is going to cost thousands?'

'I know, but this is my last hope. So this is the route that I am going to have to make right for me,' I replied determinedly.

'Right, well, let's book you in for some blood tests.'

I eat my feelings, and I have a lot of feelings, so when the doctor looked at my recent history, she saw that I had been checked for polycystic ovary syndrome (PCOS – a common condition that can lead to difficulty in getting pregnant) and diabetes in the last year. No sign of either. She saw my cholesterol was really low (apparently a modern miracle for someone who eats!) and could see no obvious reasons why I shouldn't look into it further at this stage. I felt sick. I knew that she literally could not tell if I was fertile from looking at tests for another disease, but I felt encouraged. There wasn't an 'oh, wait, you broke your nose in the nineties? No babies for you.' She told me that the bloods that needed to be taken had to be done at a certain point in my cycle and I should come back then. I didn't even ask what the bloods were testing for. I just couldn't believe she wasn't laughing at me.

I didn't want to give her the opportunity to reconsider, so I just got up and left as quickly as I could, wiping my eyes, pulling myself together. Step two of a million, taken. No roadblocks. Not yet.

Now, I am not someone who tracks their cycle, because I have never really needed to. I wasn't on the pill, I didn't suffer with my periods (not like now, since giving birth, when they take over my bloody life!), so it hadn't occurred to me that I would have to wait to have the bloods taken at a certain point. This was my first lesson that with all things fertility, it didn't matter how ready you were, you had to wait for your body to catch up with your mind. So I bided my time and waited for my period, all the while googling things I didn't understand. Like a rubbernecker at a motorway accident, I knew I shouldn't be looking but I couldn't help myself. And, like rubbernecking, my Google investigations resulted in nothing good, just more questions. I was just going to have to sit back and wait.

THINK YOU WANT A BABY ALONE? WHERE TO START?

- Look up the Donor Conception Network. They have a wealth of information on all aspects of donor-conceived children, including booklets on how to talk to people about donor conception. They have local groups that connect people in the same situation and hold conferences covering a range of donor conception topics.

- Speak to your GP about getting blood tests to check your hormone levels. If your GP is unable to offer these, look into acquiring one privately if you can afford one. Then you will know what you are dealing with in terms of your fertility possibilities.

- Search out relevant hashtags on social media and people who have written about their experiences. Respect boundaries; don't bombard someone you don't know with personal questions if they haven't invited you to do so. Ask them if they are happy to discuss it with you. #smbc (solo mum by choice) and #solomum are good starting points.

- Try to talk to your friends and family. I think you would be very hard pushed to go through parenthood entirely alone without the support of this network, so get them on board early to hold your hand when you need them to.

- Save.
- Save some more.
- Save even more.
- Save every single penny. Never have another bought coffee again, put that cash into a savings account instead.
- Have I mentioned saving?
- Be brave and patient.

This gave me time to talk to a good friend, a financial advisor about remortgaging my house to get the funds together for not only my treatment, but also some much-needed home improvements to accommodate an extra person in the house and enough money to cover a year of maternity leave. When you are going it alone, the luxury of having someone else pay the mortgage while you care for your babe just isn't there, and as I knew this was likely to be the only time I was to have a baby, I wanted to enjoy as much time as I could with them without having to juggle work, too. The finances were all going to be a real push, but we made it happen. The bank said yes, the paperwork was in place, now I just had to hope my body was in as good a position.

Finally, the time came to have the bloods taken. Even then, I didn't ask what they were for. I assumed that, you know, if your blood comes out green, then they tell you kids probably aren't something that is going to happen for you. I have had PCOS tests numerous times because I am so hirsute that Barnham would have signed me up in seconds, and I am still convinced there is a reason for it, yet the tests always came back negative, so I wasn't concerned about that. However, all the things that I didn't know they were testing for were what was worrying me! As ever when I am scared, I buried my head in the sand and didn't ask any questions for fear that I wouldn't like the answer. So I sat down in front of the nurse, shoved my arm out, looked the other way, they took the blood and I walked out none the wiser.

More waiting. If nothing else, fertility is a long game of patience and chance. I impatiently booked my appointment to pick up my results. No green blood. I discovered that, fairly obviously, they were testing my hormone levels, and it turns out my FSH and AMH levels were on the good side of average. I could now add FSH and AMH to the list of acronyms I was going to have to learn (see page 74 for more!). I could also continue to the next stage!

What the hell was the next stage, though? I knew that my GP had done all she could for me and so now I was on my own. (Sidenote: I never looked into NHS funding for my treatment – fertility resources on the NHS are a medical hot potato and it was not something I wanted to get burnt by, so I removed myself from the situation by paying privately. I was so privileged that it was even an option for me, but am acutely aware this may not be a possibility for all.) Well, I was on my own except for brilliant friends who work in the fertility industry! My friend Jenny is an embryologist, so all this was nothing new to her. Talking about fertilisation, eggs and sperm was, for her, as normal as asking what she had for breakfast. Which was a good job, as I had a lot of questions. So many, in fact, that I didn't really know where to start. So I asked her to start for me and she very patiently went through the various options.

You start at the bottom with the entry level, getting-pregnant-without-a-man procedure called intrauterine insemination (IUI), where sperm is placed directly into the uterus. It is the least invasive, least expensive and least successful treatment available. Then there is assisted IUI (IUI+), which is the same but with added hormonal drugs for a higher chance of success. After that there is the more widely known in-vitro fertilisation (IVF), a much more invasive, more expensive and ultimately more successful process that involves removing your eggs and fertilising them in a laboratory setting before they are placed back into your womb. This by no means covers the full list of fertility treatments available, but it was all I needed to know at that point. Prior to doing some rudimentary online research and talking to Jenny, IVF was the only one I had heard of. It was also the one that made me most anxious, because of the many stories I have heard from friends who have been on that painstaking journey.

While I still didn't know *how* I was going to get pregnant, the one common denominator I knew that I needed, whether I did IUI, IUI+ or IVF, was sperm. Lots of it. Or not. Who knows? Definitely not me. I had watched a documentary that summer called *The Vikings are Coming*, which was about people using donor sperm from Denmark. In fact, sperm is apparently one of Denmark's biggest exports, who knew? Donating sperm in the UK is not a common thing to do – for a start, you don't get paid. If you don't believe me, ask your male friends, boyfriend, husband or brother if they have ever or would ever donate their sperm. I can pretty much guarantee the first reaction will be some sort of facial grimace! It is rarely something they have ever thought about. However, for some reason, perhaps because you get paid, by way of compensation, for your wank, the Danes aren't as averse to it. Therefore, the pool of swimmers for you to choose from is much larger in Denmark than it is in the UK. That is not to say you cannot get it from other countries, but this documentary focused on Denmark and my friend Jenny had also mentioned a Danish sperm bank, so that was suddenly the country I knew most about, and the country I had decided was going to be my future kid's fatherland. (Let's also not forget that Denmark is consistently named the happiest place to live on earth, so that pretty much sealed the deal. And it has great bacon. Always bacon.)

So, I had reasonably good hormone levels, I had money in the bank, I knew that, somehow, I was going to get some Danish sperm and I knew the options available to me in terms of treatment. The dots were starting to join together – still not quite enough to see that the picture being formed was that of a foetus, but nonetheless that image was beginning to take shape.

I needed more information, so it was back to the only drawing board I knew: Google.

I looked for clinics in London, purely because I had heard a few pretty bad stories about my local clinic, which had put me off using them, and London was just an hour away. The first clinic I called said they would send me some information, and they duly did. This gesture was enough for me to decide that was where I was going to have my treatment done. This was, I discovered, not a great way of going about choosing a clinic. What I should have done was more research. Any research! Most clinics have open days so you can get a sense of the place before you commit to them. You can often feel pretty vulnerable when you are having fertility treatment and you need to feel safe, understood and looked after. 'Do as I say, not as I do', that's the expression, isn't it? Well, that applies to most of my fertility journey. It appears that all I needed the clinic to do to convince me to choose them for the most important medical undertaking I would ever have, was for them to answer the phone. Such an amateur.

I booked in to have my initial consultation. The more steps I took towards the end baby goal, the more giddy and ultimately out of control I felt. I still had no idea what I had to do, how much it would cost, or when it could start. Nothing. I knew nothing. I just had to wait for the meeting at the clinic in the hope they would be able to answer all my questions and address all my fears and concerns. Then something unexpected happened. My friend Dan, embryologist Jenny's partner who worked at the same clinic as her, called me to tell me they were both going to start work at a swanky (pun intended) new clinic in London headed up by a rock star of the fertility world and did I want to have my treatment there? I loved the sound of it, it made everything feel less formal, less cold, because there would be actual real people who I loved working there. I cheekily asked if they would be able to swing a discount my way, because frankly when you are paying this much money you will ask for favours wherever you can get them. The lead doctor agreed to give me my initial consultation for free, which was amazing. I was brimming with anticipation. As it was a new clinic that was yet to open, more waiting was involved for them to get up and running before I could have my appointment. I am not known for my patience, so true to form, I kept texting Dan and Jenny about when it might happen. They were so kind and never just replied with CHILL YOUR BOOTS, WE WILL LET YOU KNOW, which I would definitely have done if I'd been in their position. Then, what seemed like roughly two hundred years later, I had an appointment booked in for 28 October 2016.

Finally, the day arrived. I got on the early morning train, tingly with all the emotions. There was still the very real possibility that a fertility professional could tell me I shouldn't or couldn't go ahead. It had been four months since I had lit the green light on my plan to become a mum, but I knew this meeting could put a halt to all of it. I got a cab straight to the clinic from Marylebone and arrived in a tangle of feelings and fluster. The first person I saw was Dan. It felt so, so good to see a friendly face. He gave me a big bear hug and pointed me in the right direction. The clinic was still not quite open and was a hive of builders with snagging lists, and the smell of fresh wet paint clung around every corner. I got to reception, it felt opulent and exactly as I had imagined private London clinics to be – all white with perfectly coiffed staff. I was greeted by the professor (not any old fertility specialist for me!) and taken into his new office. It was vast. He apologised in passing that the scanner was not ready yet, so we couldn't do an internal exam today. *INTERNAL EXAM? What? Was he actually joking? I hadn't even shaved my legs. Oh my god, I thought we were just going to be talking.* Suddenly I was awash with anxiety, and whatever he was saying just sounded like white noise because I was so worried he was suddenly going to whip out some internal examination instrument of torture when I was fairly sure I had put on a pair of old knickers with holes in the early morning rush to catch the train. He was going to take one look at them and then tell me that I absolutely was not fit to become a parent.

This loud diatribe was playing out in my head while this hugely educated man was excitedly telling me about his new venture. I knew I had to pull myself together, to listen, to actually take in all that he was going to tell me. I pulled out my pocket-sized Moleskine notebook that I had bought especially (because we all know that successful projects start with new stationery) and tried to focus on asking the questions I had written down after some pretty avid internet research and hours and hours of poring over sperm bank sites. Most of the questions I had neatly written out I didn't even understand, but I wanted to sound like I was talking his language. They read:

- *Timings*

- *How do I get a sample from a Danish clinic to the UK clinic?*
- *What motility number? 20?*
- *How many do they need to have in stock? Should I buy all at the same time and store them at the UK clinic?*
- *CMV status . . . is it a problem if positive?*
- *Does the clinic need to approve the sperm before I buy it?*
- *0.4 ml or 0.5 ml?*
- *Who is my day-to-day contact?*
- *Confirm pricing*
- *THE EXACT PROCESS FROM NOW*
- *Can I use any sperm bank? Does he recommend any?*
- *Does the clinic supply ovulation sticks or are generic ones OK?*

Needless to say, I walked out of his office having wished each other well with our prospective exciting ventures and I hadn't written down one single word of what was said. Not one. He had explained to me the different treatment options, he had drawn graphs and scrawled acronyms on a scrap of paper about the decline of fertility after thirty-five, and warned me that my weight could affect things. I told him I felt that I wanted to try IUI first because I had no reason to believe that I had any fertility issues. My only issue was the lack of a naked and willing penis being in my vicinity at a specific time of the month! My issue was being single. I remember him understanding my point, but I could tell that if it were his call, he would have jumped straight to IVF because the results are better and he is a scientist. I was very clear with myself that I just didn't feel like I wanted to pump my body full of hormones when it seemed, so far, that my body was doing just fine on its own. He suggested that if I was really keen to do IUI, to just try a couple of rounds before moving on to IVF. He had a fair point, he wanted me to be able to have the best chance of success without 'wasting' money. So, because I am stubborn, he said two, I said four. That was that, the decision was made. I was going to have four rounds of natural IUI. Hopefully less.

More and more dots were being joined together. The one thing I needed that I didn't have was possibly the most important dot, though: the sperm. Honestly, I had been putting it off because choosing it, buying it, the logistics of getting it to the UK, everything just seemed so important, like they were such colossal decisions that I wasn't sure I was qualified to make them. I needed to choose the genetic heritage of my unborn child without ever meeting the man to whom those genetics belonged. I had to choose my child's donor purely via the information on an online form. I felt hugely intimidated.

After that initial consultation, I made the decision that I was going to have my first procedure in December, which gave me a month to get to know my cycle a little more and also to BUY SOME SPERM. I had chosen the sperm bank I was going to use mainly because, in fact, solely because it was the only one people had referred to. That was until I gave myself the fear that perhaps I should look further afield than Denmark. So I sourced another European sperm bank and one in the US in order to confirm to myself that the Danish route was the best decision for me. You know when you are at a restaurant, and you feel like you have made your menu choice, and then suddenly something else jumps out at you just as the waiter is on their way to take your order? It felt exactly like that. I was 98 per cent sure I wanted a smörgåsbord, but then did I actually fancy a moussaka or even a juicy burger? This meant more and more endless scrolling through websites day and night until I truthfully admitted to myself that I was just procrastinating because I was scared.

Then, a curveball. The first one, so that wasn't bad going, but a curveball nonetheless. The clinic I wanted to use was so new that they wouldn't have all their ducks in a row to carry out any procedures until January. I am not known for dealing with change well, and the thought of waiting even one extra month was just out of the question. I had made the decision that I would start treatment in December, and nothing was going to stop that from happening. Besides, what was to say that they wouldn't have another delay? Suddenly the tightrope I was walking felt very wobbly indeed. So with a heavy heart, I went back to where I started, to the clinic that had simply picked up the phone! I called to book a consultation asap, explaining that I was going to start IUI in December. They were quite taken aback because it was already mid-November and usually people aren't quite so gung-ho about it. Bear in mind, now that I had been tracking my cycle for a few months, I knew that I ovulated mid-month as expected, so my first consultation was booked for 17 November, and I hadn't chosen or shipped the sperm yet. Suddenly it all felt like there was a fire up my arse, and, frankly, that was exactly what I needed.

So off up to London again, this time meeting a friend at Chiltern Firehouse, like all middle-aged out-of-towners are taken to two years after it was The Place to Go! I remember explaining to my overjoyed friend that it was just a consultation this time, but in the next month I would be back and that time I would be getting pregnant. She and her wife were going to be trying for a baby soon, which meant she was even more intrigued about the intricacies of what I was going through and what was about to happen. We were winding each other up into a frenzy of excited anticipation for what was to come, like it was Christmas Eve.

I found the clinic and burst through the doors, noticing the gorgeous black and white floor tiles and feeling like this was it, after the initial false start, this was finally it. Reality came to slap me round the face again when the receptionist couldn't find my appointment and then tried to convince me I had another name because that seemed easier to her than working out where my actual appointment had disappeared to. Turns out she was looking at the wrong day, and my name was Olivia Thorne after all. I went through to the waiting room and in stark contrast to the crisp, clean extravagance of the other clinic, this room was heaving with as many tired brown leather sofas as the room could allow, which should have been my first indication of the business nature of this clinic – it was all about the sheer amount of people they could get to see in one day. The bland, tired sofas carried the weight of hope of both the couples and the single people sat upon them. When I walked in, a few people looked up, but no one wanted to make eye contact. You just knew that everyone in that room was going through something deeply personal, and the last thing you wanted to do was catch the eye of a stranger who was also likely to imminently be internally probed on the other side of one of the walls of this grand building. The waiting room was flanked on one side by a vast and somewhat inexplicable mural centred around a river; I think maybe it was intended to be ancient Greek in influence, with women in vast bodiced dresses and men in pantaloons surrounded by swans and cattle. It may well be a very famous piece, but classics definitely isn't one of my areas of expertise! What I did know was that it felt dated and out of place and in no way did it feel like a hopeful expression of artistry. It definitely clashed with the daytime ITV chat show on mute on the TV screen that was just a touch too small for the room. Nevertheless, this ridiculous juxtaposition somehow put me at ease.

As ever, in my pre-children life, I was nearly an hour early. I was practically moulded into the softened leather of the sofa and had imagined fertility scenarios for every other person in that waiting room before my name was called. I was met by a tall man with a thick Eastern European accent, which to me sounded experienced and therefore calming. After a firm handshake I was whisked to his office and asked what it was I wanted. I produced my blood test results and I explained I had already had a consultation, had decided on four rounds of natural IUI and that I wanted to start next month. Without so much as a skipped beat, or once looking me in the eye, he went into a full explanation about how IUI was absolutely the wrong decision for me. I was old and fat, so IVF was the only sensible option. Of course, he didn't exactly call me old or fat – rather wonderfully, the fertility world label anyone over thirty-five as geriatric (although I believe they have moved those goal posts now) and anyone fat they refer to via their arbitrary BMI number. He produced laminated graphs to back up his point, showing a steep decline in women's fertility after the age of thirty-five, which, coupled with my love of chips, meant the only answer he could possibly consider for this equation was IVF. I explained clearly my reasons for wanting to try IUI first, and with a defeated and audible huff he crossed his arms and suggested I have a HyCoSy test to assess my fallopian tubes. HyCoSy is an ultrasound procedure that I had read up about, as something I may need to look into should I discover I have fertility issues, which is intended to check my fallopian tubes were in good nick and could pass an egg, or if the problem lay elsewhere. Again, I was firmly of the belief that I did not have any fertility complications other than the fact I was shit at Tinder. I also knew that add-on tests like this were costly, usually in the hundreds of pounds.

I politely declined, at which the doctor rolled his eyes, stood up and took me through to an examination room in order to give me a transvaginal ultrasound. This basically translated as inserting a large plastic wand into my poor unsuspecting vagina and me trying to act totally normal while staring at indistinguishable moving black-and-white images, which apparently would reveal my reproductive future. All the while it was being explained what exactly was on the screen, like an audio description at a museum, but sadly set in the wrong language, as translating from medical to average-person terminology would have been bloody helpful. I had never thought about what happened inside my body, much less what it looked like, and it was impossible for me to make the words coming from the doctor and the visual on the screen correlate. There were a couple of nods, some sharp inhales and very reassuring smiles from the nurse to my right. The doctor left the room and I was instructed by the nurse to get dressed and go back to the doctor's office in my own time.

I walked back in, knickers on again, the doctor still not looking me in the eye once. He explained for my situation (old and fat) that I had an 'average to good' amount of follicles in my ovaries, twelve to the right and eight to the left. Each follicle contained an egg and, with a fair wind, one would be released at ovulation. He kept telling me that IUI had just a 10 per cent chance of success, and so, again, as a scientist he wanted to take the quickest route to success, rather than perhaps what I felt was right for me. I left the clinic with my mind made up. I think the pull of the doctor wanting me to undergo IVF so strongly actually made me acutely aware that I was going to do IUI, because I pushed back every counter argument with determination. IUI felt right. I knew what I had to do, the path was suddenly very clear. First up, sperm.

A TINY LIST OF DONOR-FERTILITY RELATED ACRONYMS

This is in no way an exhaustive list. This book would be impossible to lift if we did that. These are just a few of the key ones to start you off:

- AMH – anti-mullerian hormone
- FSH – follicle-stimulating hormone
- SMBC – solo mum by choice
- DD – double donor
- TTC – trying to conceive
- IUI – intrauterine insemination
- IVF – in vitro fertilisation
- TWW – two-week wait
- MOT – motility (regarding the motility of sperm)
- DS – donor sperm
- FET – frozen embryo transfer
- BFP – big fat positive
- BFN – big fat negative
- EPT – early pregnancy test
- US – ultrasound

I had procrastinated enough; it was mid-November and I was likely to ovulate in the next three weeks.

I needed to choose the sperm, buy it and ship it as quickly as possible to make sure it was at the clinic in good time for my first IUI. I vowed I would make my decision that weekend. I got home after work on the Friday night with a box of Magnums, a new pack of Post-it notes, some multicoloured Stabilo pens and a fresh notebook for company. I cleaned the house (procrastination, if ever I saw it!), lit some candles and started my mission.

The sperm bank website had a pram instead of an online-basket icon – it all felt so bloody unreal! You didn't need to login, you can just go straight ahead with the search, as if it is your weekly shop. You can filter by ethnicity, height, weight, eye colour, blood type . . . honestly, the list goes on. From all my research, I knew that one thing that was important to me was to have an open donor. That meant that when my child was eighteen, they would be able to contact their donor should they wish to. I felt really strongly that I wanted my child to have this option and that it shouldn't be my decision to take that away from them. I was going to make enough decisions on their behalf throughout their life as it was, and whether they wanted to introduce themselves to their genetic heritage would be entirely up to them, not me. As much as I would absolutely love to find out who this mystery hero was, to scratch the itch of my intense nosiness, this time it wasn't my call.

So once I had filled in the list of things I assumed I wanted, I just had to wait for the algorithm to do its work. Tall, blond, open donor, slim build. I figured if I was to have a choice in this, that tall and thin to counteract my short and fat seemed like a blooming marvellous idea. Likewise, it seemed sensible to choose the same hair colour as me so they had more of a chance of looking similar to me in the future. Truly, not that I in any way cared what they were going to look like, but I really didn't want my child to look so different to me without knowing who they did look like! That uncertainty would have driven me bonkers.

The first set of results came up with what I assume were fictitious names: GIDEON / BLUR / SAUL / SANTIAGO / BARLEY / RANCHER. Ask anyone I know and they will tell you I have a real 'thing' for names. I am obsessed with names that 'fit' together, names that sound kind, and quite often names that are nothing short of ridiculous. Whatever the name, whether it is Jim or Hercules, I will have an instant reaction to it. So some of the donors that came up I discounted straight away because of their ridiculous fake names. How ludicrous is that? Yet at that stage I had nothing to go on in terms of trying to whittle the list down, so I had to start somewhere. I could always try again if there was no low-hanging fruit. It was like Tinder without any of the images of men draped over cars that don't belong to them or hugging a tiger. You literally just had stats to go on to entice you into their genetic bio, so you really couldn't do a quick glance 'wheat from the chaff' type of cull, unless you brought things like fake online names into it. Which I did. The initial search resulted in so many more matches than I had anticipated, I felt like I was drowning, like I would never get to the end, and the stakes were so bloody high. It is not even as if it is a 'yes' or 'no' answer, as there was no right or wrong. It was a spermy stab in the dark at best, which actually made it so much harder.

I had previously asked a couple of friends to come over and search with me, to help me make the decision, and just to talk things through with them. It felt like a huge weight on my shoulders to take it on alone without so much as discussing the options with anyone else at all. What if I had missed something really obvious? It soon became apparent with each friend that came round that they too felt intimidated by the task, because every single time one of them left the house, we hadn't even opened the laptop to look at the sperm bank website. I think this was about the time that I really, truly recognised that I was doing this alone. On my own. Just me.

I read through the profiles with my Post-its in front of me, which had the converted heights and weights to measurements that I understood (feet and stones, if you are asking!), while slowly getting through the box of Magnums. I had been watching what I ate since the summer and had lost nearly two stone, so greedily scoffing the ice creams felt like the sort of treat I deserved for this mammoth task. Never knowingly not eating my feelings. I had also given up alcohol, which was probably best, as god knows what the consequences would have been if I was knee-deep in gin at the time of choosing. The amount of information you are given about each donor varies depending on the sperm bank, but the one I was using gave you a daunting amount. As well as giving you a photo of them as a baby, they tell you their favourite colour, childhood memory, his dominant hand, whether he has full lips, his resting heart rate, how he describes his personality, what he considers his weak side, and the list goes on and on. I suspect I was given much more than many people know (or need to know) about their other half that they have been waking up next to for nine years. You also, rather brilliantly, could read a handwritten note about why they had chosen to become a donor, which had an accompanying audio file, so you could also hear their voice. I mean, what a double-edged sword! They all just sounded gloriously intriguing because they had such rhythmic and calming Danish accents! The answers to why they had become a donor were far-reaching, with some being clear that it was for the (minimal) cash and others giving very Miss World 1984 type answers. What none of them said was that they were a narcissist, or they were Granny's best friend or mildly irritating when two pints of Tuborg in. You know, the little things that make you connect with someone or not.

Hilariously, there was also a part where the staff at the sperm bank described how *they* perceived the donor in person, which was in theory a great way of getting that 'real' perspective, but the clincher was they also, bizarrely, had to liken each and every donor to someone well known. I can't begin to describe how comical and yet futile this was, as they obviously had to choose people who would be well-known globally, rather than perhaps someone from an episode of *The Killing*. So I would say, according to the staff at this particular sperm bank, that at least 85 per cent of all their donors looked like Hugh Grant, with the occasional Colin Firth. I can't look at Hugh Grant now without visualising that infamous mug shot of him from the nineties and assuming that it was taken at the sperm bank for their files. Sorry, Hugh.

Once I felt more at ease with what information was being proffered, I started to flippantly cross people off the list for not liking dogs, for declaring *Grease 2* as their favourite film or for listing techno as the music that would get them on the dancefloor. While it was becoming pretty easy to say what it was that I didn't like about the innermost feelings of these men, I still had absolutely no fucking idea what it was that I was actually looking for them to say. What little shiny nugget of information was going to grab my hand and thrust it towards the online pram basket? I had convinced myself I would know it when I saw it.

So on I went, disregarding bios on the smallest morsel of their character that I irrationally decided didn't work for me. For a while I think I was looking for someone who sounded like they would be good to hang out with, like it was some sort of dating website. Which, let's face it, I was also shit at, so it is not like I had good form. Plays guitar? Tick. Loves dogs? Tick, tick. Fluent in three languages? *Oui, ja, si.* Could talk about food all day? Tickety McTickerson. Then it slowly dawned on me that none of that meant anything at all. It was so unlikely that any of these traits were going to be passed down genetically from the donor. My dad was a marathon runner, will you ever see me wrapped in a tinfoil cape at the finishing line of a 26.2-mile breakdown, though? It suddenly became glaringly obvious that what could possibly be passed down were any genetic health concerns. My family is riddled with cancer, amongst other things like strokes, so suddenly I didn't give a shit if this guy's favourite book was Alan Bennett's *Talking Heads*, what actually mattered was that his family's medical records didn't read like a script from a whole season of *Grey's Anatomy*. I had been searching for the wrong clues. Obviously when you go through an official sperm bank, the donors are heavily screened, so it would be very unlikely that someone that was deemed to have a 'problematic' genetic history (whatever line in the subjective sand that may be) would be given permission to become a donor, so I felt I was on pretty safe ground here.

Using sperm banks is hugely cost prohibitive. It is absolutely not lost on me what a hugely privileged position I am in that I was able to yearn for something and be able to afford to make it happen. There are so many people in my position who simply can't get the money together for fertility treatment, so they buy sperm from more unofficial channels, like Facebook. Let me make it very clear, I would have done that too, if that had been my only option for making it happen. No judgement from me, none. I would put concerns about how many donor siblings (or diblings, as it has, too saccharinely for me, been coined!) could be in the same county or even town as me to the back of my mind in order to get to the end goal. It may be that people genuinely feel that using a friend or a Facebook donor is the best decision for them. It is all hugely subjective, as with anything fertility and parenting related. What is right for one may not be right for another. I hope that goes without saying. However, I am lucky – really bloody lucky – that I could go through this in a more HFEA-regulated way, knowing that there would be screened donors that likely looked like me on sperm bank rostas. Like I said, a privilege, a huge one. This bloody difficult journey could have been so much harder if anything from my financial status to my skin colour were different, and believe me when I say, I am grateful for that every damn day.

Once I had whittled down a few more Hughs and Colins, I started to look more closely into my selected profiles, rather than just giving them a cursory skim read. There were possibly around six or seven on my shortlist at this stage. Other information given is the sperm motility. Of course, I had absolutely no idea what this meant, even though that had been on my list of questions from my first consultation, which he might have answered but I hadn't heard a thing. So I called the clinic to ask. Essentially, it is the engine of the sperm, how fast it can go! For me, this instantly evoked *Look Who's Talking* opening-scene vibes of sperm actually racing each other. Probably fully kitted up with saddles and everything. Anyway, it is low sperm motility that can be the cause of male infertility, so if you are buying, you want to get the good stuff. I, possibly naively, assumed that if the sperm bank had it available as a 'product' that it had been screened, and therefore any of the donors listed would have a 'good enough' motility for a successful pregnancy. Likewise, you can choose how big you want the straw of sperm to be (I mean, for the love of god, why call it a straw? That is NOT the image you need in your head when thinking of sperm!). Again, my assumption was that of course you would not be given too little so that a pregnancy was impossible (although, I truly wouldn't put anything past the greed of some of the fertility industry).

I decided to discount these more technical aspects of the decision process; if I found The Perfect Donor and they had a lowish motility and only a 0.4 ml straw available, so be it. Decisions everywhere you turned; decisions needed to be made. Colossal ones. They also had to be made by someone who had absolutely no fucking idea what they were doing. Me.

So the list was getting shorter. Like a personal episode of *Blind Date*, I was asking them, 'So Chuck, what's your name and where do you come from?', while I also greedily waited for answers to irrelevant predetermined sets of questions. A mixture of Our Graham and the voiceover guy from *The X Factor* giving bellowing précis of each candidate in my head. I was seconds away from creating a jingle for each one. I was beginning to lose my mind, although it could have also been some sort of delusional sugar high from Magnum consumption.

Contestant Number One, please come down . . .

BORJE from Denmark

Driving fast cars gives him a spark

Sperm motility count of 20 (the doctor says that should be plenty)

His grandad died at 102

Solves his problems by making home brew

Listen, I never claimed to be Keats, more like a Daphne and Celeste lyricist. I just knew I had to try to make light of the actual epicness of this decision because the alternative would have been too mind-blowing and, again, there is no right or wrong answer. (I did know that there was a no-refund policy, though.) And yes, I am absolutely the sort of person that laughs at a funeral while simultaneously crying so hard I feel I might be sick.

Finally, forty-eight hours, a few episodes of the *Gilmore Girls* and nearly two boxes of Magnums later, I was down to my last two candidates. For obvious reasons, I am not going to say exactly what it was that made me finally make the biggest decision of my life, but I will say it was a culmination of familial health, a couple of keywords that made me feel like he wasn't a total egomaniac and the fact that he sounded the total opposite of me in every way. I figured I needed his yin to my yang – depending on which end of the nature versus nurture debate you sit on.

So, I had done it. I had chosen the donor for the longed-for fruit of my loins with nothing more than a hopeful wing and a prayer. I moved my mouse over to 'add to pram' (I will never get over that being their shopping-basket icon), but *fuck me* if I didn't need to make YET MORE decisions. Honestly, fertility and parenting is nothing more than a series of luck and decisions to be made. Did my clinic accept donor sperm from my chosen sperm bank? It was something I was sure I had checked, but obviously before I wafted over mounds of cash, I realised I should probably just confirm they were on the 'approved' list. Did I want the sperm shipped over in dry ice or nitrogen? For the love of god, why is that my decision? Surely, *surely* there is an optimal way to send it and therefore that must be the only option? I chose the most expensive option at that stage – in for a penny, in for thousands of pounds. You don't want to finally choose the Mac Daddy of donors for his hyped-up sperm to then need a disco nap on the way to the UK because I didn't want to spend an extra few euros for a Doctor Who'esque mode of transport. Much like when you do an online supermarket shop and as you are checking out the site gently asks if you have forgotten any items that you have previously bought. You instruct it that you have completed your shopping – another page of tempting products you don't need flash up on your screen: ARE YOU SURE, MISS THORNE? Like this could be the last time I could ever possibly buy some Marmite, so they need to be convinced I have enough stocked at home.

So, just as I think I have completed my online sperm purchase, another question. Quantity? How many straws of sperm (that will never be an acceptable phrase!) are you wanting to purchase? Christ, I need another Magnum. Breathe, Liv, don't forget to breathe. How many straws I wanted wasn't as easy as it sounds. Unlike supermarket shopping, I didn't have a recipe to tell me that I would need exactly one 7g sachet of yeast to make this bun oven-ready. If I didn't buy enough then there were two possible shitty scenarios. The first being that if I had to buy more straws, I would have to pay the shipping and admin costs again (and let me tell you it is more than a first class stamp). The worst possible scenario, though, was that I might decide to get more straws from that donor and he would no longer be available or he would have reached his positive pregnancy quota for the UK (like I say, it is heavily monitored) and then I would have to choose another donor and frankly there aren't enough Magnums in the world to get me through that. On the flip side, if I bought three straws and all the fertility luck was shining down on me and I got pregnant on the first go, then I would have 'wasted' two straws and the price tag attached to them, which could equate to a month or two of maternity leave. Or I could have stored the straws at my UK clinic in case I should want a sibling down the line. Guess what? That costs too. Nowadays clinics often do three-for-two packages and things like that, which might have helped me decide, but when I had my treatment, no such offer existed. You bought one straw for one treatment at cost. In what can only be described as my delusional state, I opted to buy three straws. I say delusional because I had, in fact, already decided to have four rounds of IUI before moving on to IVF, should they not be successful.

This is exactly why I shouldn't be left alone to make big decisions! Yet there we have it, an online pram with three straws of grade A (possibly!) Danish sperm with my name on it soon to be winging its way across borders in its own liquid-nitrogen duvet, awaiting its arrival in London to emerge through the icy vapours like the opening of a Beyoncé tour. Sperm me up, Scotty. Let's do this.

CHAPTER 3: VAGINAL STEAM, ANYONE?

I got an email from the clinic in Denmark to let me know that Order No. 641015 had shipped and that I could track it via UPS. I'm not sure exactly how I thought they were going to send my precious little swimmers from Aarhus to London, but I think I had just assumed it would be something more exciting than UPS. A white knight on a handsome steed, maybe? Regardless, they were on their way.

The time had come. I was going to get pregnant. Wasn't I? It was happening. In the lead up to this day it had dawned on me that throughout our lives, starting in our school days, we are constantly taught how not to get pregnant. Condoms being placed over bananas in front of an audience, where half were nervously giggling and had no idea what was happening and the other half were rolling their eyes so hard that you could almost hear them hit the back of their skulls. In fact, I moved schools so often that I am not sure I ever had one sex ed lesson. What I did learn, though, was that you absolutely did not want to get pregnant. Heaven forbid. It was never really discussed what one might do should one find oneself in the extraordinary position of actually wanting to procreate, other than to just have sex. Keep the banana, get rid of the condom.

Even when I decided to try to get pregnant at the grand age of thirty-seven, the only thing I knew for sure was that you needed an egg and some sperm. I had never thought of the precise timings that come with such a seemingly simple recipe. A bit like making a meringue – it should be easy. How hard can it be to make some egg whites and sugar bake in an oven? Turns out, quite bloody hard. Some people go full Mary Berry and the meringue comes out perfectly first time to the wows of the crowd over the loud hum of the ubiquitous KitchenAid, gifted to them on their wedding day, of course. Others follow the recipe to the letter, concentrating at every stage, yet nothing can prepare them for the flat, brown crispbread that awaits them when they open the oven. Then someone remarks casually, 'Oh, didn't you spoon in the sugar one by one? You need to spoon in the sugar.' You can also add cornflour and a splash of vinegar for that sticky, chewy centre. You can also keep the baking paper in place by dabbing a little of the mixture on all four corners like edible Pritt Stick. However, if your oven is not calibrated properly, there is a chance your simple mixture may not turn out as expected.

Either you know all this stuff and you emerge triumphant from the kitchen, meringue glinting like snow, or you don't. Same goes for getting pregnant. Some people get pregnant on honeymoon without really so much thought about it, because that is just what was supposed to happen. Some people have to try for a few months, or for years, some never have any success, some have numerous tragedies along the way. Like I said before, fertility is like rolling the dice; is luck on your side or not?

I was told by my clinic to call them straight away once I started ovulating and they would make an appointment for me to have my treatment the next day. That way they would have time to wash the sperm ready for my IUI. *Pardon me?* They are going to be doing what to the sperm? Why on earth would you wash it? I had just paid a shit ton of money for those little Danish swimmers, surely they should arrive ready to go with sparkling clean tails?

Apparently not. The contents of the sperm straw had to be washed in order to – and you may want to sit down for this – separate the sperm from the semen. That's right, to separate the sperm from the semen. SPERM AND SEMEN ARE NOT THE SAME THING. I still can't believe that I never knew this. I thought they were just words describing the same goods. Like boobs and tits. Pudding and dessert. Father Christmas and Santa Claus. Chips and fries. Sperm and semen.

Nope, it really is true that every day is a school day, and never more so than when you dip your toe into the giant sea of fertility. So my precious sperm had to be washed in order to separate the healthy, speedy sperm from the rest of the semen sample in order to make sure those that are inseminated are only the shit-hot ones. The real corkers. That way there is more likely to be a successful pregnancy – you know, should all the stars actually align at the same time.

Next up on my huge fertility learning curve was becoming familiar with my menstrual cycle. As I have mentioned previously, I had never tracked my period. Why would I need to? Honestly, I was embarrassingly naive about it, considering I had been having them since I was eight years old, when I discovered to my horror that my mum's sanitary towels were not in fact used to make her knickers more comfy. All I knew was that they came with alarming regularity, they were fairly annoying, and then they went again . . . until the next time, which apparently was about a month later. I had never registered that there was a time in the cycle that I would have a killer headache, that I could eat all day and not feel full, that I would have insomnia, that I would be irrational, that I would cramp. I truly just thought those were things that happened, never ever putting two and two together. Like I said, embarrassingly naive.

So when my consultant asked me how long my cycle was and did I ovulate around the usual time, I looked at him like someone in the *Mastermind* chair who had absolutely no idea what John Humphrys was talking about. But instead of just replying, 'Sharon', like the viral video clip, I think I sort of weakly agreed with him and stated that, yes, I had a pretty normal cycle. After that meeting I started tracking it avidly. I downloaded a billion apps, desperate for my period to start so I could get going. Again, fertility never just falls into the manufactured time frame that you have created, you have to wait for your body to catch up. So in the last few months of 2016, I tracked my period and it turns out I do have a pretty normal cycle. I ovulated on day 12, according to the Google doc I had created to store various notes about what I was finally discovering about the inner workings of the body I had carried around for thirty-seven years. It also turned out that the headache, the insomnia, the greed, the aches, the bad back and the anger were all related to my cycle. No shit. My period was an original, menstrual, basic bitch.

The next thing I realised – that apparently everyone in the world knew apart from me – is that the egg-white type of discharge that I would feel every once in a while actually happened every month and it was my body announcing that it was just about to ovulate. It is called cervical mucus and is the most fertile kind of mucus, I'll have you know. I mean, how sexy is that as a description? Thank god I was going this alone, it meant I didn't have to announce to my partner, 'Darling, the cervical mucus is here, come and ravage me.' It quickly dawned on me that there is absolutely nothing romantic about fertility! In fact, any subject where the term 'mucus' is used with as much regularity should ring alarm bells. Maybe that is why they don't go into fertility in any depth at school. If there is a banana near you, put a coat on it, then you won't get pregnant. End of discussion. No educational chat about cervical mucus, thanks.

For three or four months, on around day 9 of my cycle, I had started weeing on ovulation sticks even though I didn't need to, as at that point I had not yet even bought the sperm. I just wanted to feel in control, I wanted to feel like I knew what I was doing with the bloody sticks. Not that you can go too far wrong, but I still wanted to make sure I had the upper hand (even if it was covered in my own wee). These magic wands are the ovulation equivalent of a pregnancy test. Anyone who has had to use these digital sticks will be able to tell you the sheer anguish, frustration and hopelessness tinged with an air of excitement that these little plastic bastards come with. You can buy non-digital ones, but frankly I had clearly discovered my woeful lack of insight into my own body, so I thought it best to make sure I used apparatus that I knew would physically spell things out – even to someone as naive as me.

So, each time day 9 rolled around, I would lay out the stick and its holder neatly on my bathroom chair every night before bed, so as to remind myself to wee on it in my early morning half-sleep. You are advised to take the test in the morning because that is when the sample is strongest. Romantic. I'd wake up and the first thing I had to do was wee on the stick, then wait to see if it produced a little smiley face. More often than not it didn't; it produced a face with a straight line for a mouth. A mouth of disappointment.

It is wild how much emotion this tiny stick brings with it; every straight mouth it produces brings a nagging doubt deep in your soul that you have left it all too late, that you will never ovulate again and you will never have the honour of growing a baby inside you. Every morning, first thing. Even if you knew you were testing way too early, 'just in case', you would still never look at that digital face rationally. The first time the little smiley face appeared I was so bloody thrilled. *Oh my god, I am ovulating,* I thought, as if that was something my body hadn't been doing all on its own without all this pressure for the last twenty-nine years.

Practising with ovulation sticks, however daft that sounds, was just one of a long list of things that I experimented with pre, during and post treatments. I started by giving up drinking and trying to lose weight. I am pretty good at abstaining from things entirely, because I am a stubborn Taurean, but what I am not good at is moderation or will power – because I am a greedy Taurean. The only way I would be able to maintain a healthy weight was if I could cut out food altogether. My weight was the one thing that the medical notes kept listing as 'a problem', alongside my age, so I just tried to be more mindful of my diet. It is not that I eat chips all day every day (although I would, happily); I have an averagely healthy diet and am a good cook. I eat lots of fruit, veg and grains and I prepare all my meals from scratch, yadda, yadda, yadda. My downfall is the emphasis on the word 'lots'. Despite having lived on my own for most of my adult life, I absolutely cannot cook for one person. I find it almost impossible. So I will 'make enough for the freezer'. We all know that the second portion has never reached the freezer. I eat well, I just eat well for a family of four, so my plan was to try to eat a little less in order to lose some weight, continually reminding myself that apparently with every half stone I lost, my chances of getting pregnant would improve. None of this was breaking news to me, obviously, despite my naivety in other aspects of the whole getting-pregnant game.

One thing I could control much better, though, because I could totally abstain from it, was alcohol. So, again, to try to get my 'geriatric' body into the best condition I could without becoming an entirely different person, I decided to give up drinking. I wasn't a huge drinker anyway. I had decided years ago that I wouldn't drink alone at home because of my inability to moderate myself, as before I knew it, I would have been drinking a bottle of gin through a straw watching *Home & Away*. So I just extended that rule to not drinking when with friends. I am a horrific binge drinker – nothing for weeks and then as soon as I am with people, I am like a woman possessed, GIVE ME ALL OF IT AND MAKE IT A DOUBLE! Then I would spend days (a day longer with each passing year) recovering from my hangxiety. So giving up alcohol was probably a really good idea at that stage anyway.

Now I had given up drinking and I was losing weight, what else could I do to help prepare my body to accept these Danish sperm with open arms? Another good fertility fact is that the egg actually chooses which sperm she will allow in. Unlike the notion that we are taught that the sperm are racing to the egg in a winner-takes-all type of battle, in actual fact the egg has already decided what type of sperm she will 'allow' to enter. She is not a submissive egg, she is an independent woman who chooses her own destiny! WHO RUN THE WORLD? However, I did want to give her as good a chance as possible to be able to accept her sperm of choice and carry on with the baby-making journey successfully, so I looked into what else I could do to help me get pregnant.

Holy hell! Talk about Pandora's box. I may as well have searched for how many blades of grass there were in the world! The search results were endless, confusing and pretty often subjective.

One thing that came up consistently was acupuncture. My sister is an acupuncturist so I know how brilliant it can be; I'd had it before for shoulder pain, but I had never thought about it in terms of getting my body ready to welcome a baby into its fold(s!). At that time, fortuitously, a good friend of mine was seeing an acupuncturist who specialised in fertility, so I made an appointment. I am not going to claim I have any idea how acupuncture works or even exactly what it is, what I do know is that it apparently can help with increasing blood flow and energy to your reproductive organs. I also know that I bloody loved it. Every second of it. I think people just see the needles and assume it is some *Hellraiser*-type of torture, yet you very rarely feel the needle go in. I totally fell in love with my practitioner. She had the most amazing way of making me feel at ease and just knowing I had an appointment would make me feel calm. I would quite often fall asleep during my treatment and I honestly felt like I could take on the world after every session. I would say around four months before my first IUI I had acupuncture weekly, and they were my favourite forty-five minutes of the week, by far. If I won the lottery, I would have a full-time acupuncturist living with me, no question. Of course, I have absolutely no idea if this treatment actually helped me get pregnant physically, but for the impact on my mental health, I can honestly say it was the best thing I could have spent my money on.

On a local Facebook page, I also came across a woman in my village who offered pregnancy massages. While I wasn't pregnant, I contacted her anyway to see what she would recommend. Ultimately, she was a skilled masseuse, so what on earth would stop me wanting to hop onto her table amongst the whale-song noises and neroli scent wafting around her front room? I am not someone that would get giddy about a day at a spa – the thought of stripping down to my undies while someone wipes their oily hands all over the soft folds of my body is actually something that makes me recoil! I would always dread the hen party that revolved around white dressing gowns and a series of 'treatments'. I would almost, *almost*, rather be at a strip joint in Piccadilly Circus with a penis tiara. However, what I did know was that despite jovial appearances I am a chronically tense person. My physiotherapist sister has always commented on how tense my body is. When I hurt my shoulder years ago, I went to the doctor to see if I had done any actual damage, and he felt around my neck and declared that he had 'never really felt muscles this tight'. If only that had been a good thing! I was well aware that a tense 'on guard' body would probably not be one that would find getting pregnant easy. Your body needs to be willing to accept those sperm and not automatically see them as intruders, standing there with its arms crossed at the cervical border. So I made an appointment to have the ninety-minute massage. Ninety minutes! There is no way I wouldn't fart in that time, like the laughing in church reflex. Also, some stranger touching me – for ninety minutes! I was dreading it. Ridiculous, but true.

FIVE WAYS TO GUARANTEE A SUCCESSFUL PREGNANCY

1. There are none.
2. Do not trust anyone that says they can guarantee pregnancy.
3. It is called the fertility INDUSTRY for a reason.
4. Fertility is an inexplicable, heartbreaking and magical lottery.
5. Have I mentioned there are no guarantees?

Searching for the key to unlock successful fertility was a constant maze of 'my friend said this helped' and 'I saw an article about xxx'. Truth is, there is no answer. There is no one reason why for some people it is as simple as having drunk sex one night with a guy you fancied at work and for others it is a constant dark emotional struggle that steadily chips away at their very being. If you are in the latter group, there is very little you won't try in order to get pregnant. You need to lick a toad at the stroke of midnight on a mountain in Czechia to stimulate healthy egg growth. Eating six broad beans a day and washing them down with an organic apple cider vinegar margarita will ensure sperm are at their peak. Need the perfect uterine wall thickness? Easy, just stroke the forehead of a Tibetan monk during a leap year while snacking on well-massaged kale and you will be just fine. In all seriousness, though, if you are desperate to get pregnant, you are exactly that, desperate. You will try almost anything, and unless it sounds obviously harmful, you are game. Which may go some way to explaining why I gave myself a vaginal steam.

There is no rational explanation for this act other than Gwyneth Paltrow is a fan, so it made the news and therefore I heard about it and thought, why the hell not? Surely a steam-cleaned vag is the perfect environment for an egg and a sperm to lovingly run into each other's arms? Like I said, you get desperate, you try anything. I hadn't even had one IUI treatment yet and already I was listening to Gwynnie for The Answer. I lined a bowl with rose petals and other ephemera before pouring boiling water over it and waiting for a few minutes before I sat astride the bowl. What. The. Fuck. Seriously, what the fuck was I doing? (It's worth noting that apparently this practice is not to be encouraged and I never did it again.)

Anyway, I went for that massage, and while I wouldn't say I totally enjoyed the experience, I knew that I felt terrific when my clothes were back on! My body felt amazing. Actually, that is a total lie, I felt like I had been pummelled by someone needing to let out their frustration. Then, a couple of days later, I felt totally dreamy. As ever, who knows if it was something that would iron out the creases that I thought were in my body, making it ready to accept a baby, but it definitely couldn't do any harm.

So far, so generic; massage, good foods and acupuncture. While I don't think it did me any harm physically, I am not sure how many of my remaining marbles were taken in the process. I really just wanted to get pregnant and where possible I didn't want to inject myself with hormones until I knew I had to.

Often, from nowhere, I would be bowled over with the enormity of what I was trying to do. Like the infamous *Only Fools & Horses* sketch where Del Boy leans on the bar only to discover it is not there, I kept thinking I had my shit together and would relax about the whole process, then I'd lean on that metaphorical bar only to realise that someone had opened the bar hatch and – THWACK – I hit the deck mentally.

Oddly, this never, ever, not once, formed any anxiety about whether or not I could physically and emotionally be a one-parent family. I was so very sure that it was something that I would thrive at, that I could nurture a child, that it was definitely something that I was meant to do. No, what would floor me would be the thought of going through fertility alone. Just me. It seems lunacy to think that this was what was worrying me more than a lifetime of parenting single-handed, but my fear of taking the fertility journey alone was absolute. This possibly irrational feeling had properly ignited while I was trying to choose the donor; however it pervaded everything that came after that, too. The intrusive internal exams alone, the travel to the clinic alone, no one else to listen to the information given to me by the medical staff while my mind wandered. Just me. It was truly daunting.

Yet despite all this, it was still a solo mountain that I longed to climb, to be able to stake my flag in the summit, even though that summit seemed like a long bloody trek away. How long, though, was still tbc. Which in turn made the anxiety flash through my veins. I am very, very bad at not being able to plan or feel control over defini- tive actions that need to be taken at an agreed time. You know when friends may flippantly say things like, 'Yeah, let's meet around 7.30 p.m. and then we can decide where to go for dinner'? A sentence like that could spin me out for hours. Around 7.30? Around it? Why? Can't we just say exactly 7.30, on the dot? Or am I going to have to aimlessly wander around the agreed meeting area in the hope that we get there at the same time. Hoping people don't assume that I am hanging around on my own with nothing to do and no one to meet? When anxiety con- sumes you, you often cannot fathom a world that isn't centred around you. So you think everyone in a restau- rant will be staring at you trying to find your friends and you assume they think that because you can't find your friends you are a bona fide twat. Actually, the chances are, they haven't even seen you, and they quite literally do not care that you are there at all. So, if I manage to get over the mental hurdle of a loose time arrangement, I am then entirely preoccupied with the fact that not only do I not know where we will be eating dinner, but I also have no idea at what time this will be happening. So many variables are out of my control in this situation, that this sort of casual approach to meeting up can sometimes veil any rational judgement I have and will culminate in me making my excuses to bail. I was on a date once, which I arrived at about an hour early for fear of having to walk through a pub while looking for someone I had never met before, knowing, on this occasion, that they actually *were* likely to be watching me. Half an hour after we were supposed to meet, the guy gave me a call asking where I was. I told him I was in the pub we had agreed. So was he. Just on the other side of the bar. He'd got there about two hours early for the same reason. We were both quite pissed when we met! Needless to say, it wasn't the start of something beautiful, when perhaps it could have been had my wall not been so high.

So, as I set off on this next part of my challenge, the sheer number of moving parts to getting pregnant and trying to get them to work together was what was causing me the most angst. Little did I realise that once I had actually had a baby, very little would ever truly be in my control again!

Vagina steamed, sperm en route and a vague notion of my ovulation cycle and I was ready, probably, for my first treatment. Suddenly I wanted to feel like one of those women who never had a hair out of place, who had a specific section in their handbag where they kept their lipstick and who wore heels like they were truly comfortable. I booked a hair appointment, I was waxed from head to toe (literally!) and had my nails painted in Rouge Noir, because as a nineties teenager, Mia Wallace was, and will always be, the epitome of cool to me. I bought new underwear and had picked out an outfit that seemed appropriate for getting sperm thrown up my uterus. I cleaned my silver Vans. This was serious.

Now I just had to wait. Wait for the fucking digital smiley face. It was December, my very favourite time of year, which is why I had pushed to get going at this time, and because I thought it would be a great romantic tale to tell about getting pregnant at Christmas. However, no amount of schmaltzy Channel 5 Christmas movies was speeding up my eggs. Time was almost at a standstill. The butterflies in my tummy, growing by the day, were now nearly hawk-sized. My advent calendar (that I bought for myself, because I dive head-first into the festive season with jingle bells on) took on a totally different meaning. Yet I had no idea what door I was waiting to open. I just had to be patient and accept that proceedings were out of my control, which as you now know is not my forte.

To help me get through this (hopefully) fertile journey, I decided early on to tell all my friends, family and colleagues what I was doing. Apart from wanting to share my story in the hope of normalising donor conception, I felt really strongly about talking openly about hoping to get pregnant from the moment I made the decision. The thought of not knowing when my treatments would be because I was at the mercy of my body; I literally didn't have the energy to make this all more complicated than it already was in terms of the lack of ability to plan anything. Also, I am crap at keeping things I am excited about a secret! Telling everyone what I was doing meant there was never a time when I would have to hide my feelings or make excuses for my whereabouts. Especially when it came to work – in that case, my time wasn't my own, I was contractually obliged to be somewhere, and of course I couldn't give notice that I was not going to be in the office – just twenty-four hours in advance, if I was lucky. My clinic was in a different city to me, so it is not like I could just pop out at lunch and have my treatment. So I was very grateful with how understanding all my colleagues were. Above all, perhaps selfishly, it was also much, much easier for me that everyone knew. I was so fortunate that on the whole everyone I cared for couldn't have been happier for me, or more supportive to me in what I was doing. Not once did anyone hesitate in reaction to my plan with a doubtful look plastered over their face. That is, until I opened up the conversation online. Then some more, shall I say, 'ill-considered' responses were offered up, but very, very few.

DAFT THINGS PEOPLE WILL SAY TO YOU IF YOU HAVE OR ARE THINKING OF HAVING A DONOR-CONCEIVED CHILD

- Could you not just have a one-night stand?
- Will the baby look like his dad?
- I was probably going to do that if I hadn't met Dave.
- So is it a designer baby? Can you choose what you want?
- How much does it cost?
- Will they be yours?
- Why not just adopt?
- Will you tell them you didn't know their dad?
- I don't think I could ever do it alone. Are you sure you want to?
- Are you pregnant yet?
- Oh, I know exactly how you feel. Dave has to work away three days out of seven.
- I am single-parenting this weekend because Dave is at a stag do.

Then, finally, it came. The smiley digital face. It was there. Grinning away in the candlelight of my bathroom (I am not Emily Brontë, I just hadn't changed the bulb) was his pixelated face. Fuck. This was it. I called the clinic, fizzing with excitement. The fizz soon flattened. This is perhaps when I realised that I had definitely chosen the wrong clinic for me. Although, maybe the clinic I needed doesn't actually exist. It's funny, the fertility industry is totally polarising in terms of how people perceive it. You either had a great experience and you can't recommend somewhere highly enough. Or not. I was the latter. I called, not knowing where the anticipation ended and the excitement started. 'Sorry, we don't have you registered. What's your name again?' After spelling my name a few times, confirming that I'd had an appointment there in person recently, that I had used my life savings to send semen samples to them that they had confirmed were in their storage facility, and reassuring them that I definitely wasn't born in 1987, they were able to certify my existence. Computer no longer said no. This was followed by more accusations: 'Well, how do you know you are ovulating? Are you sure?' Oh god, maybe I had been doing it wrong, but the consultant said I did not need scans at that stage and that the sticks would be enough. 'Oh. Really. Let me see,' she said, harshly. I honestly wanted to vomit.

I knew it was coming. I knew it was there, the open bar hatch, I had been waiting for it this time, I was braced for impact. This was all going to royally fuck up. I felt tears prick my eyes and my throat tighten. 'OK, yes, apparently we do have your sample here and we can see you if you really do think you are ovulating.' I exhaled so loudly my breath bounced off the phone and hit me back in my own face. We made an appointment for the next day.

In my need to control the situation, I drove halfway to London and then hopped on the train to Marylebone. It was peak Christmas party season. It was only around 11 a.m. and yet the carriage was full of M&S pre-mixed cocktails being gulped down loudly and the air was thick with sweet perfume. I couldn't get my head around the fact that these people were off into town to throw their company profits down their necks before the inevitable argument on a dancefloor, cheeky snog and dirty kebab on the last train home. Yet, before they had even got to the first course of their pre-ordered starter, I would be alone in a doctor's office, legs akimbo, trying to make my dreams come true. The huge disparity was blowing my mind. I wanted to tell them how excited I was. I wanted to join them and down one of those double-shot M&S gin & tonics so badly, to ease my nerves. Then we chugged into Marylebone. I didn't know which plat-form we would arrive at – sometimes it stops at one so far away from the main station you may as well have got out at Slough and walked in. Mind you, I had time on my hands. I had, of course, picked a train that would get me into London about two hours before my appointment. Just in case. Perhaps I really just wanted to study the ridiculous mural on the clinic wall some more. Either way, I bade farewell to my train buddies and we went our separate ways – them to get drunk, me to get spunk.

Arriving at the clinic was slightly like an out-of-body experience. You know when some days you just cannot believe you are an adult? That you are someone who is responsible for things like pay-ing council tax and having smear tests? Surely I couldn't be grown up enough to enter a clinic on my own in order to have fertility treatment? Surely that was something that was happening to someone else? Nope. It was me. I was the adult. Half expect-ing the clinic to still turn me away and for this to fall through, I walked up to the reception that was squeezed under the grand staircase with a very con-fident stride, so that the uber-glamorous receptionist could tell I meant business.

The building felt familiar now, and when I entered the waiting area crammed full of its worn, brown leather sofas (do not picture beautifully aged Chester-field-type leather sofas, this was the bank holiday sale 1993 type of leather sofas), I didn't feel like the new girl at school. I didn't feel lost at sea this time. I waited patiently, scrolling through my phone yet not being able to concentrate on anything that was happening on my screen. I went about creating the life stories of the other people in the room again. I do this a lot; I invent worlds I think other people live in. Probably giving them much more excitement than their actual daily life usually afforded them. By the time my name was called, it was all I could do not to hug the couple sitting opposite me, who I had named Willa and Doug, and the scenario I had created for them for being in that crumbling building was so heart-wrenching that it was ripe for a *Guardian* weekend feature article. (God I would love to know why they were actually there!)

I beamed at the nurse who had called my name, des-perate for her to like me, for her to really want me to get pregnant, and to urge the doctor to 'make it a good one' and take a bullseye shot first time. As we walked further and further into the depths of this cavernous building, I was babbling away more and more and

I could tell she was getting out of puff and disinterested. My heart was sinking with every step we took. Why weren't we bonding? Why wasn't she responding to my inane chat with reassuring kindness? She was probably used to the verbal diarrhoea of anxious women before their inaugural fertility treatment. I wasn't any woman, though. I was me. I really wanted this to feel special somehow, for my getting-pregnant story to have really warm, non-sterile memories. Let me tell you, that wasn't happening.

We finally reached the room and the nurse kicked into her version of the air travel 'emergency exits' speech. It felt like it was all off a script, nothing sincere, nothing bespoke. It was at this point I realised that she was going to be doing the procedure. My consultant was nowhere to be seen. Obviously I had never done this before, but I had foolishly made the assumption that the doctor I had spent piles of cash on in exchange for his time, knowledge and reassurance, was not in fact a person I would never see again but would instead just be a name at the top of my clinical files. While I know full well a nurse is more than capable of doing a job they have trained hard for, that wasn't my concern, I was just shocked that again I had made assumptions that turned out to be totally false, and that I was immersed in something that I knew less about than I thought.

As I re-emerged from my thoughts about the absent doctor, I realised the nurse was talking to me. Her script had got to the stage where she was asking me to confirm my details. Then she pointed at a test tube. THE SPERM! There it was, cold and sterile in its little metal stand. I had to confirm that the details on the tube and the details on her piece of paper were a) the same, and b) indeed the sperm that I had purchased. I confirmed this was the case. Borje was the donor and this, I presumed, was his sticky DNA.

With my signature scrawled across the relevant pages, the nurse instructed me to get ready and excused herself from the tiny room. Bless her for thinking I had enough dignity left to need her to be absent while I removed my knickers, when in a few minutes she would be delving deep in between my thighs. Regardless, she left, I removed my knickers and placed them neatly in my handbag, like a grown-up would, and jumped onto the cold bed. I say jumped, it was more a heave and a shuffle at this point. Re-entering the room, it seemed that the nurse had read my mind and it felt like she was trying to be more cheery. My gran would have called her a 'homely-looking' woman, so it felt jarring to me that she wasn't all warm smiles and comforting chit-chat. The IUI procedure is nearly exactly the same as a smear test, except there is no scrape, instead there is an injection of something that feels a little cold (the sperm!). As I have always been diligent about having my smear tests regularly, I was used to the speculum, the hand-held metal or plastic device that is inserted into your vagina to separate the walls so the doctor can inspect inside your cervix and/ or vagina. Just another feature in the long list of the truly glamorous aspects of being a woman. So from extensive experience of this device, I warned the nurse that I was likely to break the speculum.

'You are not going to hold it, Miss Thorne. You can't break it,' the nurse replied.

'No, I know, but when it is inside me, I will tense up and I will break the speculum.'

'Oh, no you won't, don't worry, that has never happened before, you will be fine,' she said confidently.

'Sure, I know I will be fine, but I'm just letting you know I always break it.'

I could tell she was desperate to roll her eyes at me. I then went on to inform her that I had a tilted cervix, so she may need to reach a little further back. I felt like the person ordering a hamburger, but without the bun, or the relish and could they possibly serve it cold, with lettuce instead of chips?

'That's good to know. Now spread your legs apart and relax.'

Sure. This was wildly relaxing. Someone I met five minutes before had their head up my vagina while they inserted a large plastic duckbill into me, as I lay marooned under glaring strip lights. Even though I knew what was going to happen next and even though she had been warned what was going to happen next, we both let out gasps of astonishment when it did, in fact, happen. Seconds after inserting the speculum, I tensed up and the hinge that keeps the two parts held together flew into the room. PING! I thought now might finally be the time we bonded. I had broken the bloody speculum. Surely that was worth a cheeky titter?

'Well, I will have to go and get another one.'

The nurse left with the separated pieces, one in each hand, and a face of bemusement. OK, cool, now she was actively annoyed with me. She returned with a smaller speculum and we started again. I knew it had worked this time because I could feel the cold of the sample hitting my insides. Then the speculum was removed and the nurse started to take off her plastic gloves. I couldn't believe that was it. All over. Had it not been for the broken speculum, it would have been over in ninety seconds, despite my tilted cervix getting in the way.

'You can stay there if you want. When you are ready, get dressed and make your way back to reception with your notes. Oh, and here is a list of do's and don'ts and our contact number in case you have any questions.'

'How long should I wait until I do the test?'

'Well, you can't do it now, you have only just had the procedure. You will have to wait two weeks like everyone else.'

'Oh yeah, I know not now, but I was just checking on the two weeks. Should I ring you to let you know?'

'Only if it is positive, we have to make a record. Bye.'

Literally like the worst date ever. I lay there in that sterile room, feeling a little sad and a little used, oddly. I know it was a clinical setting, of course it was, but I hadn't expected to feel quite so . . . clinical. I think I just thought I would bond with the nurse and it would be a fun five minutes, all things considered. But no, it was paperwork and broken speculums. I lay down for a little while, but actually I just wanted to get out of there. I got dressed and tried to retrace our steps through the maze of the ancient building back to the receptionist, all the while doing Kegels to try to make sure gravity wasn't releasing any of my precious cargo.

'I think I need to hand you my notes and pay for my treatment,' I said to the receptionist when I finally made it back to where I'd started.

'Yes, that's right.' She smiled. 'Let me check. Oh yes, you need to pay for your storage too. That is eleventy billion Great British pounds please and eighty-five bronze pennies.'

She typed in the figure and thrust the card machine at me. My PIN almost reflected the cost. In that moment I really just wanted to be at home. I felt a little flat and wished I could click my heels and be back in Oxford. The traipse back to the station, the wait for the train, the jolting train journey and then finally the car ride to get me home all seemed to take an absolute age. I wanted to feel something; to have a flutter of pregnancy, even though I knew that was both impossible and ridiculous. It really was similar to leaving a date you had looked forward to with the nervous excitement that was quickly turning into the disappointment of reality when you discover they are actually married. You feel a little silly and a little helpless, cross that you had convinced yourself you were expecting something that was never on offer, even though it is possibly your fault for misreading the signs.

I got home and lay on the sofa, wishing someone was there to hold my hand. Elvis, my dog, was giving me as much love as he could muster while still being livid with me for having left him with my neighbour all day.

If you have ever tried to get pregnant by any means you will know the dread of the 'two-week wait'. This is how long you have to wait between sex/treatment and taking a pregnancy test. It is a black vortex of time. There is absolutely nothing you can do to make those two weeks go any faster. Not even at Christmas when the days usually whizz by as there is so much to do and so much going on. Not even the promise of a Terry's Chocolate Orange or a boozy drinks party can speed them up. After what felt like roughly sixty-three years, and having aged considerably in that period, the test day had dawned. I had, as does everyone, really wanted to test early and yet I knew that would only breed its own form of uncertainty, however many lines the test produced. So I diligently stuck to the rules. I had bought some biodegradable shot glasses that I was going to wee into. I knew that if I just pissed on the stick as required, I would convince myself I hadn't done it correctly, so

I had decided to fill three or four shot glasses instead. I had also bought two sets of tests: the first was an expensive digital test that would spell out whether I was pregnant, rather than leaving it to the mercy of my possible misinterpretation; the second was a packet of some regular, cheap-as-chips tests. I KNEW these would be exactly the same as the expensive ones, but marketing had suckered me in again. Well, marketing and a touch of desperation. So, shot glass one housed the jazzy digital stick and the others cradled the simpler ones. I waited the allotted time and doubled it, just to be sure. After the two-week wait, the final ten minutes seemed like a breeze.

not pregnant

While I trusted the test implicitly, I still checked the others. Same finale. I wasn't pregnant. I knew I wasn't.

Suddenly everything was really noisy, the dog was barking at the postman, my head was exploding with sadness, my alarm was going off and the dull December daylight seemed to sear my eyes. Despite being convinced that I had no fertility 'issues', I started scare-mongering myself that actually I had, that this had all been a totally fucking ridiculous idea all along. Who was I to think I could have a baby alone? I was thick with a cold and I couldn't work out if it was making my breathing feel tight or if it was just sheer desolation. I felt numb. It was 30 December and I crawled back into bed, alone. Fuck.

I can't remember if I called him, if he could envisage my patheticness telepathically or if he was sent by my sisters, but my nephew drove down from London to de-Christmas my house. I always did this on New Year's Eve, so that the house felt fresh and new, ready for exciting times ahead. Yet this year, I didn't feel any excitement at all, so doing it a day early wasn't going to hurt. Having a cold meant that I could translate my emotional feelings into physical ones and could convince myself and everyone else that it was the average winter sniffles that were making me feel so rotten. I sat on the sofa while my nephew took the decorations off the tree. The hug he gave me when he arrived had left an imprint on my body because it had felt so good to be held, to not feel alone. Luckily for me, unlike some twenty-three-year-old boys, he is very astute and empathetic and knew his sad old auntie would love to be hugged by all six foot two of him for a little longer than he would have liked! I was so grateful for him that day.

I never go out on New Year's Eve, I hate the forced fun of it, the fact that everything is twice the price and that I will wake up the next day feeling shit and anxious.

So usually I stay at home, clean the house, change the sheets, cook a juicy steak and placate Elvis, who is shivering from firework fear. My friends are much more likely to want to go out to celebrate, but as the majority of them have children now, that has made it infinitely harder. A few years before, we all started going out for lunch on New Year's Eve instead of seeing the new day and new year in, which made it feel like we were still celebrating somehow. It was always a massive kerfuffle of a meal, the type where you feel really sorry for the staff because you know that it is almost impossible to serve us. Not because we are being rude, but because there are about sixteen adults and 41,697 children, which must be the hospitality equivalent of hell. That year, it also felt pretty rubbish for me too. In hindsight I shouldn't have gone, but I was so determined to show that the negative test had not affected me that I thought it was imperative I turn up. The noise was intense and being surrounded by kids felt like rubbing vinegar on an open cut. The real clincher was that of my two closest friends there, one was eight months pregnant and one had just announced she was expecting her third. The emotions I am all too familiar with surfaced. The acute tension of being thrilled for people you dearly love and feeling a deep hollow ache of jealousy and longing. I don't remember for sure, but I can make a guess that I would have left early, making excuses about the dog and rushing back to the warm, quiet security of home.

The raw disappointment started to ebb away as I knew that I would imminently be ovulating and I could try again, so I tried to pour all my energy into feeling excitement instead of despair. I thought that perhaps having someone with me at the clinic next time would make me feel less anxious. The trouble is, when you cannot give people a definite date and time until twenty-four hours in advance, it is bloody impossible for anyone to commit to coming with you. Luckily one of my best friends is her own boss, with children at school, so she could be pretty flexible. She agreed, excitedly, to come with me. It felt so good knowing that I wasn't going to be alone this time and that the endless clinic corridors would feel more familiar.

The digital smiley face appeared on the LCD screen one mid-January morning. This time when I phoned the clinic, they didn't interrogate my identity, they could see I existed! It was snowing and the M40 was filled with that strange light that comes with snowfall in England. Leila was driving carefully, knowing that I was ready to put my foot on the non-existent brake in my passenger footwell at any given moment. She had lived in London for around fifteen years, so navigating the busy streets to our destination was second nature to her. The A40 transformed into busy London roads and suddenly we were outside the clinic. We sat amongst the now-familiar sea of brown leather and wondered what other people in the waiting room assumed our story was. Again, I was arrogantly believing that people were paying far more attention to us than they actually were. My name was called and we made our way to the woman standing at the front of the waiting room. This time, it wasn't my original doctor or the nurse I had seen last time, but someone new entirely. She was one of the founding doctors at the clinic and was reading through my notes with assurance. She was much more up for a chat than my original nurse, which, along with Leila being there and knowing what was to come, made me feel so much more relaxed. As she was talking to us, I knew I recognised her accent as it was soothing and familiar to me, so I, possibly rather rudely, asked to know where she was from. Was she Iranian? Yes! I knew it, and the reason I knew? Because Leila, lovingly standing beside me, was Iranian too, and there are very few things in the world that comfort me like her mother's voice. They talked of Tehran, food and family, and suddenly that clinical room felt like it was much warmer. I signed the paperwork and got into position. Leila at the head end, obviously!

'I see you have a tilted cervix, so this may take a little longer than usual while I find the right spot.'

'No problem, I know it is a little trickier. I am also likely to break the speculum.'

'Ooh, how exciting. Let's see how we go with this one and we can get a smaller one if needed. Ready?'

'Yep.'

I gently squeezed Leila's hand, so grateful for her presence, but that was not the only thing I squeezed! PING! Off went the speculum. Of course it did, I have internal walls of iron ... The doctor swiftly left the room and came back with another and we started again.

'There. All done. Rest as long as you like and I will meet you at reception when you are ready.'

The whole experience was just so different to the first time. It felt familiar and I took the Iranian connection as an inexplicable sign that this was definitely going to be The One. Buckets of cash transferred, I was chauffeured back down the M40. I was heady with excitement and the familiar feelings of butterflies returned. Now I just had the epically long two-week wait to contend with. In January, already the month with 291 days too many.

HOW TO GET THROUGH THE TWO-WEEK WAIT

- First, be kind to yourself and acknowledge that this is likely to feel like at least two years rather than two weeks.
- Try to have at least three or four things to look forward to in that time, like dinner with (understanding) friends, going to a gig or having a haircut.
- Save up all your shit to-do lists and do them in those two weeks, like writing thank you cards, returning your ASOS packages, renewing your car insurance. Anything to keep your mind busy.
- Non-strenuous exercise is good during this period, so go on some long old walks with a gripping podcast or audiobook.
- Write. It. Down. Everything you are feeling. Write it all down. Not only will this feel like therapy it will be interesting to read a few – less raw – years down the line.
- Flick anyone really hard on the forehead who says, 'It'll be fine, don't worry' or 'Is it test day yet?'

In all honesty, I don't remember the details about that two-week wait, the taking of the test, seeing the not pregnant screen, having the next treatment and its corresponding two-week wait and the crash of disappointment that would come with yet another not pregnant. I have an incredible (albeit possibly not wise) ability to shut out periods of trauma from my life. Yet I know that is what I was going through. Emotional trauma. The only real, tangible moment I can remember from that time was tinged with as much joy as it was deep heartbreak, in that my darling friend had her longed-for second baby. I was called in the middle of the night to go and look after my goddaughter while her mum and dad went to hospital for their new arrival. I was so excited and nervous about telling Molly when she woke in the morning that Mummy was having the baby, but I just could not, for one second, believe that would ever be happening to me.

Molly and I busied ourselves during the day and waited. Molly more patiently than me. This was happening two days after I had taken my second negative pregnancy test. My friends weren't being insensitive, they knew I wanted to be able to help, to be involved, however much it felt like my maternal craving was becoming more and more unlikely to be satiated. Finally, we heard the news that everyone was well and that Molly had a baby sister. I took her to the hospital to see her mum and dad and to meet the little baby that was making her a big sister. Little Molly suddenly looked so very grown up. We all cried, for both the same and for very different reasons. I left the fresh family of four and went home. Alone. I remember the smell of hospital followed me home, with what felt like a constant reminder of what was not on the cards for me.

I had unsuccessfully used up all three of my sperm straws that had been waiting on ice at the clinic. Gone. No baby. I had nothing left to give. I simply couldn't go through this one more time. Not yet. Not now. It would have been easy at that stage to talk to the clinic about IVF, which is what they had wanted me to try from the start. It would have been the perfect time to talk about the next steps, what with no straws, no baby, no third time lucky. But I had told myself that I would have four rounds of IUI and so I was going to have four rounds of IUI. One more shot. The bullseye. But not now, not yet. I would have a month or two off to recover mentally from the colossal weight of raw disappointment that was cloaking my tender body.

The elephant in my spermy room that I was trying to ignore was the fact that I did not know if my donor had any more straws available. It was the thing that would make me sit bolt upright in the night with terror. What if he had reached his successful pregnancy quota? What if there were just no more samples left? There were not enough Magnums in the world that could allow me to imagine the fear that would unfold in my head at having to go through that choosing process again. Not even the Double Gold Caramel Billionaire ones! So I ignored the problem. February went by, March, April, May. If this were a film, there would be a time-lapse showing a bare tree starting to show its first flush of spring leaves and blossoming into the full green plumage of summer by the time I had removed my head from the sand and decided to log on, one more time, to see if my Danish hero was still throwing me a life raft. Borje was still there! I couldn't fucking believe it. That was it, my mind was made up, all systems go. I bought one more precious sample straight away and told the clinic it was on its way. This time was different, though. I genuinely, truly, didn't for one second think it was going to be a success. Yet I simply had to go through with it, because those were the rules I had given myself. Four rounds. No more, no less.

So as soon as I had made my purchase, I sort of forgot about it all. I didn't care what outfit I wore to the clinic, I didn't get waxed, my vag wasn't steam cleaned (I only did that the once!). I was still having acupuncture because I loved it and I still wasn't drinking because I was enjoying the absence of that too, but other than that nothing had changed. I even decided not to get involved with the ovulation sticks because I truly never wanted to see that blank digital face ever, ever again. I didn't see the point in buying any more when I wasn't going to get pregnant and I now knew when I was ovulating. With the regularity my body had shown me over the last year, the cervical mucus appeared and I knew now was my time. I called the clinic, booked my appointment and drove up, all the way up, to the clinic on my own. No fuss, no drama, no expectation.

THE EPIC PLAYLIST I LISTENED TO ON THE WAY TO MY LAST TREATMENT

I am not saying it worked, but it is epic . . .
(You can find a link to the Spotify playlist at www. livsalone.com/playlist)

- 'I'm Not Going to Teach Your Boyfriend How to Dance with You' – Black Kids
- 'The Rabbit, The Bat and The Reindeer' – Dr. Dog

- 'The Whole of the Moon' – The Waterboys
- 'The Pieces' – Slow Club
- 'Two Doors Down' – Mystery Jets
- 'I Feel for You' – Chaka Khan
- 'Graceland' – Paul Simon
- 'How Long Do I Have to Wait for You?' – Sharon Jones & The Dap-Kings
- 'No Diggity' – Blackstreet
- 'Simply the Best' – Tina Turner
- 'Ain't No Mountain High Enough' – Marvin Gaye & Tammi Terrell
- 'Passin' Me By' – The Pharcyde
- 'Me, Myself & I' – De La Soul
- 'Regulate' – Warren G
- 'Kick, Push' – Lupe Fiasco
- 'Little Bit' – Lykke Li
- 'First Love' – The Maccabees
- 'Human Touch' – Bruce Springsteen
- 'Do You Remember the First Time' – Pulp
- 'Father Figure' – George Michael
- 'Thirteen' – Big Star
- 'Hey Love' – The Delfonics
- 'Baby' – Donnie & Joe Emerson
- 'Into Your Arms' – The Lemonheads

- 'Thinking About You' – Radiohead
- 'Oh Me' – Nirvana

I arrived ten minutes before my appointment and got comfy in the brown sofas amid some building work that was taking place. Guess who called my name?

The nurse from my first treatment shuffled slowly through the corridors, apologising for the building noise, and further and further through we went to the treatment room.

'Is this your first time?'

'No, it is my fourth. You have treated me before.'

She opened the door for me to enter, looking me up and down presumably to see if she recognised me.

'Oh, did I? I see so many, I forget.'

'No problem.'

I started to take my knickers off, folding them up to put them away. She went through the script of verifying who I was and if the test tube was that of the donor I had shipped over from Denmark. I signed the documents and lay on the bed as she went out of the room to get gloves.

'I'm likely to break the speculum, by the way.'

'Oh no, love, that never happens. You will be fine.'

PING! Speculum broken. Smaller one retrieved. Sperm in. Knickers back on. Cash handed over. Back down the M40, via Burger King for the first time in honestly about ten years because I was so hungry. I got home, hugged the dog, went for a walk in the meadow behind our house and then lay on the sofa to watch *Parks & Recreation*. I felt nothing, I was just pleased I had got the fourth round out of the way and I could start to plan my next steps. Whatever they may be.

CHAPTER 4:
WOOSH, WOOSH, WOOSH

This time the two-week wait didn't seem to drag on for as long as the others. Time hadn't stood still. I knew I wasn't pregnant, so I didn't have to hold my breath for those fourteen days in anticipation of how my maternal life may unfold. I had my weekly acupuncture the day after my treatment, as usual. Not because I thought it might help with a pregnancy, but because it had now become my favourite day of the week! My acupuncturist told me my pulse felt very strong this time. Of course it did . . . I wasn't feeling anxious about my pregnancy results because I wasn't pregnant, so my body was just in a state of blissful relaxation. My body and I were in sync for the first time since I had decided to prod it, probe it and chuck a stranger's sperm into it. We both knew that there was no expectation on us at the moment. We were on a break.

Although it was the height of summer, I found myself standing in a field surrounded by people and yet on my own, knee deep in thick wet mud. For the last ten years I had gone to the same festival with the same group of friends because it was local, intimate, cheap and usually had a cracking line up – always headlined by a band that reminded me of my heady days when I was pretending to be a DJ, like The Lemonheads. When we first started to go, there was a huge crowd of us, and I would dance in the fields in my wellies into the early hours, to dirty drum and bass, while talking to strangers and swigging a flat, warm, gin and tonic mix that I had decanted into a two-litre water bottle with a dash of squeezy lemon. Honestly, I am rarely happier than when I am drunk in a field, in the small hours, dancing to music I never normally listen to but in that moment suddenly feels like the primal beats of my very being. As the years went on, the decanted warm booze of my past turned into over-priced single-shot gin and tonics, with ice, in a glass, that I had to queue for. Waking up with a hamster-cage mouth on a sweaty yet freezing tent floor became me paying my niece to collect me from a field in the middle of the night so I could sleep in my own bed and wear my hangover cape of shame alone. Same-same, but oh so very different.

That summer, though, I found myself in that familiar field on my own. The last woman standing. This time I had no intention of drinking, as I had still not touched a drop for around a year, and even less intention of staying. I was going solely to see The Libertines headline, as Pete Doherty owed me a full set from when he walked out of a London gig two songs in in the early noughties. That, and a good friend was there and she had asked me to bring her some dry socks. Like I said, times had changed.

The weather was biblical; the sort of mud that, unless you have the confidence of being two litres of warm gin down, you have to really concentrate on your centre of gravity in order to keep upright. It was dark and the light of the fairground rides and food stalls was reflected in the oozing muddy river that had replaced the grazing grasslands, giving off a fairly magical yet fucking freezing glow. I stood on the edge of the main crowd, desperately hoping no one would brush past me, as I was convinced I would immediately lose my footing and fall face-first into the mud, which was no doubt 67 per cent bodily fluids at that stage. It felt like a film scene where the lead character stands stock still in the middle of Times Square while life, lights, movement and chaos pans around them in full technicolour. I was warm and clean and sober and old. So very, very old. I found my friend (a colleague who is a good fifteen years younger than me) and handed over the package of dry socks to her. Long gone were the days when I was being handed bags of weed or bottles of poppers in misused agricultural land. No, now I was handing over socks. Thick, warm socks. God, I wish I could have given her more, like a lift home to a clean loo and a hot bath. It was then that I realised that I had already turned into a mother. There may have been no life growing inside me, but while my friends were at home tucking up their kids and I was in the field with which we were well acquainted, filled with years of booze-blurred memories, handing a young girl some dry socks, I knew my time had come. I had crossed over from exuberant general admission to an AAA lanyard that I didn't want to feel the weight of round my neck anymore. I drove home halfway through Pete's set. This time I had walked out on him.

I had taken some time off work, so I went to Bristol to stay at my brother's house with my nieces. My brother was away, so it was just us girls and, of course, my ever-faithful, ever-present, ever-anxious Elvis.

Although it had just been a couple of days since I had been knee-deep in gloopy mud, the weather was now tropical. I always feel like I am on holiday when I am at my brother's house – whatever the weather. I've no idea why this is, perhaps it's the abundance of food and booze and the fact that outside my bedroom window is a palm tree and view of the estuary. This time it really did feel holiday-like because the heat was intense.

My nieces were looking for a new flat and had booked a viewing, so one morning we drove through the steep streets and winding roads that surround the city, and while they viewed flats, I walked Elvis. Both he and I were uncomfortable in the heat and after a while we sat down in a small park under a tree for some shade. Not once did I stop to think about the fact that the next day I would be able to take a pregnancy test because now the two-week wait was up once more. In fact, I am not sure I had even thought about taking it at all for the whole time. On the way home from our unsuccessful flat-viewing trip, with Elvis and his thick old dog breath on my knee, I had my head edging out of the window. The car seemed loud on the road, and the heat inside it was making me feel queasy. It was also the sort of sickness I get when I am hormonal, so it was nothing for me to be alarmed about. That drive – with my niece's little yellow car darting around those corners, up and down those roads, the windows open, all of us talking at the same time and Elvis panting furiously on my lap – will be one that I will never forget.

After a great night's sleep in my favourite bedroom in the world, I woke up still feeling a little pukey. Again, this was not unusual, so I didn't think twice about it. The bathroom at my brother's has the best shower in the world and I wanted to feel its warmth over me as soon as I woke up. As I was getting ready to hop in, I spotted a pregnancy test in my overnight bag. I knew I could take it today and I probably should – even though I wasn't pregnant – just to make sure everything was normal. I didn't have my plastic shot glasses with me this time, so I just did it like everyone else does – with a steady hand. Once I had done the test, I laid the stick on a little loo-roll rug I had made for it, because it seemed the right thing to do in someone else's bathroom, while I hopped into the shower. Freshly clean, I got dressed and went upstairs to get breakfast with the girls. I don't know how long it was between when I'd weed on the stick and all over my hands and remembered to check the test, but I would definitely say around an hour. It just went out of my mind. I was too excited to be chowing down on Marmite toast made from the most delicious sourdough from my brother's cafe in town.

And then . . . *HOLY SHIT! The pregnancy test!* I couldn't believe I had forgotten it. It seemed odd to care so little about it, when the past three times it had felt like I was treating that plastic white stick as if it were the very embryo itself. Now it was lying abandoned on some loo roll in a bathroom that wasn't even mine. I took myself off to my bedroom. At this stage, my devil-may-care attitude was disappearing fast and the familiar feelings of tingling anticipation were surging up inside me. I walked into the en suite and picked up the stick from the shelf behind the loo.

pregnant 2-3

What? Wait. What? I read those eleven characters over and over again. I wasn't pregnant. I knew I wasn't pregnant. I hadn't even taken the ovulation test. I hadn't got someone to drive me up to the clinic. I hadn't painted my nails. I hadn't steamed my vagina. There was no way it could have possibly worked. Not to me. No way on earth.

I sat on the bed. Bewildered. Slightly panicked, if I am honest. If I was pregnant, I wasn't supposed to find out here, I had always pictured finding out in my bathroom at home. That is what I had planned. My mind was loud and chaotic; disbelief and excitement so tightly entwined that they were cancelling each other out and I was just feeling, well, numb. How could I possibly be pregnant? I stared and stared at the stick.

pregnant 2-3

I ran out of the bedroom and shouted up to my nieces. The house is open-plan and upside-down, so the bedrooms were downstairs. One niece was in the kitchen upstairs and ran to peer down over the bannisters to see what I was holding up. The other skidded out of the shower she was in, dripping wet and trying to wrap a towel around her as fast as she could. The next few minutes are now a blur; I think there was a lot of hugging. A lot of screeching. A lot of gasps. A lot more screeching. Tears. Hugs. Screams.

I decided to take another test, to make sure the posh one wasn't lying. We waited. This time the wait was real – it felt like an absolute age. My body was being taken over by that sick feeling from the day before. OH MY GOD! It was morning sickness I was feeling. It wasn't the heat and Elvis's breath. It was bloody morning sickness. Morning sickness. Me, I had morning sickness. Because I was pregnant. We looked at the other stick. There were two very clear blue lines. OH MY FUCKING GOD. I WAS PREGNANT! My mind and body were full. Of Marmite toast, of disbelief, of shock, of excitement, of nausea . . . of a bloomin' baby. There was a baby inside me. I was literally flooded with feelings and crushed by hugs.

A couple of minutes (although it could have been hours, I have no recollection!) later, my nieces left my bedroom and I sat down on the bed to try to work out what the fuck was happening and what I had to do next. Should I be telling someone now? Should I call the clinic? Elvis was sat in the corner of the room, looking anxious. The preceding screeching of excitement had put him on edge. I went and lay down next to him, gave him a hug and had a little cry. At that moment I could have slept for days, possibly years. I was exhausted. The angst of getting pregnant and wondering whether it was even a possibility for me was slowly ebbing away to allow new fresh anxieties to build up in my head. What if those pregnancy tests were wrong? What if I lost it? What if it was triplets? What if I couldn't cope? What if I was a shit mum?

I wouldn't allow myself to be as excited as I truly wanted to be. I wasn't good at letting go of my emotions, I knew all too well from a lot of experience that when you had everything you ever wanted it could all be taken from you in a second. I just wasn't comfortable allowing myself to be swept away by joy and happiness at what my future might just be now. Instead, I was looking for the problem. The part that would break my fragile heart.

I knew that as soon as I started to tell people, this would all feel so much more real. I FaceTimed all my siblings. My brother and his wife were beside a pool on holiday in France, with my young nephew demanding to know if it would be a boy like him. One sister was out for a walk in a field with her children and was as shocked and thrilled as I was. My other sister took my call outside the kitchen of her deli by the sea, with a grin so wide it contorted her face. Their pride and delight was infectious, and just talking to them and seeing their raw emotion seemed to give me permission to feel it too.

I. WAS. PREGNANT.

All I wanted to do was talk about it. I was giddy. My nieces' friends came over for lunch and suddenly, as quickly as I had let it all go, I had to rein it in! I couldn't tell these young girls my news before I told my friends. Also, why would they care? Yet it felt so very odd that I had just found out that my whole life was going to change drastically, for the better, and I was asking people I didn't know to pass me the salami. Oh god, was I even allowed to eat salami? What are the rules?

WHEN TO ASK SOMEONE IF TREATMENT WAS SUCCESSFUL . . .

- Never.
- If they are pregnant and they want you to know, they will tell you, until then, it is not your business.

The sun was beating down, it was unpleasantly hot for me, a winter worshipper. I had no sunglasses and the white walls of the house felt like they were boring into my very being. I remember thinking that I should probably get some good sunglasses, now that I am a mother. I called one of my best friends – also my business partner – soon after to let him know. He was so thrilled for me, and once more I rode the wave of other people's excitement while I slowly tried to allow my own to be real. I didn't want to tell my girlfriends over the phone. I wanted to tell them face-to-face. One of the few perks of fertility treatment is that people don't tend to ask you if it is successful. They wait to be informed, and if no one heard anything from me, it was assumed that I'd had another unfruitful round. So it wasn't odd at that stage for me to proffer no information and for them to ask for none in return. Anyway, as well as myself, I had convinced everyone that I wasn't pregnant this time, so they were not anticipating hearing anything different.

I should point out that I feel a huge fraud when I talk about fertility 'treatment' because, in the grand scheme of things, I had no actual treatment. I had a very simple procedure, despite the broken speculums. I was poked and prodded, yes, but I was not pumped full of hormones, I did not have to have invasive surgery, I did not have to use both egg and sperm donations, I did not have to fly abroad to see medical professionals, I did not go through this emotional turbulence for several years. My experience was akin to a fairly straightforward house sale – putting an offer in on a house, having it accepted, a date set, contracts exchanged and the completion day arriving as expected. Of course, the process was not without hassle, but happily there were absolutely no shit surveys, broken chains, haggling over damp treatment costs, six-month waits, disappearing solicitors and no lack of available removal men. So yes, I had been to a clinic and people had rummaged around my internal organs but my 'journey' was a short one and I am always very aware of that – and grateful for it, too.

I drove home from Bristol the next day, desperate to get back to sort stuff out. I have NO idea what I thought I was going to be able to sort out when I was just hours pregnant, but I just knew being at home would calm me. Looking back, this was a vaguely comical notion because everything at home was less than calm. I was having building work done. Actually, I wasn't. I was supposed to be having building work done, which was supposed to have finished weeks ago and yet my house still wasn't even fully closed off from the elements. I had always thought that horror stories about rogue builders were a bit far-fetched and nothing could be that bad, but my god, I know now. This guy had done a number on me. I was having a simple one-floor, one-room extension in order to make the house a little more usable with the hope that a baby would soon be crawling around it. A job that should have taken two months, tops. He disappeared after six weeks. Essentially, a bigger job had come through, so he just thought he would up and leave. He texted me to say he had decided finishing the job wasn't worth his while. It had already gone way over budget and way over time. He had two guys that helped him who said they would finish it for me. Of course, the costs went up and my hands were tied because no reputable builder would want to come and finish off half a job of a charlatan. I was livid, but tired.

The last year was really taking its toll and fighting it seemed like it would just protract things even further. So when I say I just wanted to be at home, actually I would rather have been anywhere else, but, as ever, my need to be in my own surroundings was magnetic.

Over the next few days, I surreptitiously made arrangements to meet friends, so that I could tell them face-to-face without arousing suspicion. At each encounter I would pass them my phone and ask them to look at an old photo of my mum. Then I would instruct them to keep scrolling to the next image, which was of the positive pregnancy test. I have no idea why I did it like this. I think because, face-to-face,

I really found it hard to say the words 'I am pregnant'. It still felt like something that happened to other people, not to me. It felt fraudulent somehow. It also felt fucking fantastic. I was finally being allowed a glimpse of what it was like to be the adult I had always wanted to be. Sure, I was living alone in a building site and not on a farm with a hot, doting, rugged partner, but I was living the dream. I was pregnant.

I cannot tell you how often that phrase went around my head. It felt so alien. As if I had made a grammatical error that didn't sound right. Reiterating it to myself to allow myself to believe it. Tears were shed, gasps of joy, admissions of disbelief. The more and more people I told, the more I chipped away at the wall of uncertainty I had built in my head. I was finally beginning to accept that I had created my own fairytale. The other thing cementing my belief that this was, in fact, very real, was the sickness. Holy shit, the sickness. It was truly all-consuming. Like everyone else, I mainly knew of morning sickness from cute little scenes in rom-coms where the beautiful but shocked pregnant woman would suddenly be sick, much to her astonishment, just once in the morning, and then that was that. Just one little puke and their beautiful life would resume. I call bullshit. The person who coined the phrase 'morning sickness' is the same evil bastard that professed pregnancy was nine months long and the ratio of weekdays to weekend days should be 5:2. My sickness was at all hours of the day and night. Sickness, but also tiredness. The effect that pregnancy had on my body was shocking to me. I had just never assumed I would feel *this* bad.

During those first few months, I had a lot going on in my life. In addition to trying to get my head around the fact that I had managed to make my dreams come true and if I was really sure that was a good idea, I was also in the midst of setting up a company with some friends in order to be in control of our own time while also doing more of what we loved. God knows, if I was to be a single mother, I would need to have some degree of control and flexibility over my own time. So all in all, it was a tense time, not made any less tricky by the fact that I would need to throw up or, worse, *feel* like I needed to throw up every twenty minutes. I was also still living in a building site. Never have I needed to be in my own surroundings more, but it would have been great if I didn't have to share those surroundings with builders.

Every single little thing would set my sickness off. I asked the builders to smoke at the end of the garden, and yet still I could feel the plumes of smoke entertaining my nostrils and travelling down to my stomach and leading me to the bathroom floor, if I could make it there in time. Usually, I loved the smell of smoke, as I used to smoke heavily. I was thoroughly good at it. I excelled at it, in fact. I wasn't an ex-smoker who would balk at the whiff of a Marlboro Light, I would inhale it with vigour. As ever, though, I was all or nothing, and about ten years before, I had decided that cigarettes had to be in the nothing column, for fear I would turn into Dot Cotton. Yet now, sat upstairs in my bedroom with my laptop perched on my lap while I lay in bed – because there was nowhere else to work – I could smell someone having a cheeky ciggie a mile off.

Pregnancy also blessed me with irrational fears towards certain foods. Normally, there are very few foods in the world I can't abide; raw onion, offal, dill and poached salmon are top of that list, and yet suddenly this list was vast. Not only vast, but inexplicably I would think about foods that weren't even near me or on the menu and I would be sick at the very thought of them. I became obsessed with my hatred of cottage pie. Can you imagine having any feelings towards cottage pie other than to greedily eat it on a winter's night? I had started to buy frozen meals as cooking was becoming trickier and trickier due to the aromas, and sat in my freezer was a one-portion cottage pie. One night I sat bolt upright in the small hours, my mouth drowning in its own saliva and my teeth tingling, knowing that any second now I needed to be near a loo, all because I had thought about the cottage pie in my freezer. In my sleep. A cottage pie I wasn't even eating. Honestly, it still makes me shiver now, so etched in my brain is this memory. The next morning, I explained to the builder exactly where it was in my freezer and asked him to take it home. He thought I was bonkers, but he happily accepted his free meal.

We had our company meetings in a local hotel (we had decided not to get an office as it seemed to be money we did not need to spend at the time. Fast-forward to March 2020 and the fact our business worked perfectly well remotely was a blessing we didn't know we needed!), which wafted out the most intense air freshener to cover up the smell of the clandestine meetings I am convinced were a regular thing within its four walls. There was nothing that would trigger my sickness quite like that smell. The boys I work with had no idea what I was talking about as they couldn't smell it, but to me it took over every sense in my body. The meetings were not helped by my tiredness, either.

This would wash over me just as fast as the sickness did. Again, one minute I would be having a chat about marketing strategies and the next I would wake up with my face attached to the coarse, hard-wearing fabric of the banquette seating in the hotel cafe. The boys didn't say a word; they would just allow me and my body to do their own thing without once making me feel like a twat. I was, and still am, so very grateful to them for that. I mean, they were probably scared I would throw up on them or something, so leaving me alone seemed the best strategy to them, but still, I am grateful.

At home it was just as bad. One day, a neighbour found me asleep on my gravel drive, in the rain, because evidently I wasn't able to make it the final three feet to my front door. I can't explain the ferocity with which pregnancy and all its side-effects took over my body. I had paid good money – really good money – to feel this shit. I had done this to myself. In addition, the building works had gone from bad to worse, and in September, when it should have been finished at least four months previously, at the latest, I couldn't handle it anymore and moved in with friends, then my sister and her family. Feeling so ill in other people's houses is far from ideal. You already feel like you are a bit of a burden by being there in the first place no matter how welcoming they are, and then you have to ask them not to spray that perfume/please don't cut that onion until I am out of the room/can we eat a little earlier tonight? Or they find you asleep in the car on their drive. It is just not how you expect things will be when you are in the first throes of pregnancy. Unsurprisingly, there aren't many movies about this.

On top of the sickness, the exhaustion, living with other people, never-ending building work and a new job, there also seemed to be this bizarre pressure of feeling like you shouldn't tell people you are pregnant because you are not yet twelve weeks. I have always struggled with this notion that pregnant people are almost expected to embrace, but I thought it was something that I couldn't really comment on because it was not something I had ever lived with. Yet now I was living with a pregnancy, I still really didn't get why you were expected to keep hush-hush about it until you had your first scan. I don't know if it was because I was doing it alone, but I felt, and still feel, that should something go wrong, I would want that support bubble around me. I would want people to know, without having to explain to them that I was pregnant and that now I wasn't, to help me to normalise the fact that not all pregnancies end up with a baby, that it is heartbreaking, and to show people they are not alone. I would want them to come and hold my hand. I would want them to give me space if I asked them to. I would want them to know that I was hurting. I would want to be excused from the meeting with no questions asked. I would want them to know so that I had the option of asking them to leave me alone or to hold me close.

I strongly feel that the choice of when to tell people you are expecting should entirely be that of the pregnant person. They should tell people whenever they want to, not wait until twelve weeks because that is 'what is done', what is expected. Of course, I didn't want to announce it on social media until I was ready, because going that public is entirely different to telling those you love and cherish, who would support you wholeheartedly in any way possible. So I continued to tell all those people close to me that I was pregnant from the minute I found out. This was news I had been waiting all my life to share.

I truly believe that not telling people about your pregnancy in the early weeks is really about making it easier for them to not have to have a difficult conversation with you, should something painful happen. Shockingly, one in four pregnancies end with miscarriage, and yet so often women are still suffering silently, as if they should just carry on like they had a bit of a cold. There is then the expectation on mothers to go about their daily life, into work, to birthday parties, to the supermarket, to weddings, hiding what is happening to them. Whether this be morning sickness, exhaustion or if they are silently suffering a miscarriage. The episode of Fleabag that showed her sister having a miscarriage in a restaurant toilet was so raw that I wept like a baby when I watched it. The poignancy of the writing in juxtaposition with the expectation of comedy just made it gut-wrenching to watch. The character realised she was having a miscarriage in the toilet and then briskly returned back to the dinner table to carry on an already deeply awkward family meal – and it was based on a true story.

I am not suggesting this is how everyone reacts, or that if everyone round that table had known it would have been any better. However, miscarriages are often depicted as dramatic, rush-to-the-hospital type of affairs. Whereas I know (not from personal experience thankfully, but through friends) that sometimes it isn't dramatic at all. It is the opposite of that. It can just happen, when you are on a bus, or in a meeting, or at dinner with your family, and you are expected to quietly deal with it and get back to life like nothing ever happened. I knew that should something awful happen during my pregnancy, I would want, would need people to know so they could support me. It is such an emotive and subjective subject. If you have been affected by miscarriage and would like help, please get in touch with Miscarriage Association, www.miscarriageassociation.org.uk

When you register your pregnancy with your doctor, I cannot tell you exactly what to expect, even though I have lived through it, because everyone's experience seems to be different depending on your local health service and even your GP. What happened for me was my measurements were taken, along with my blood pressure, etc., and suddenly there was a huge blue file slammed down in front of me. I don't remember the details because I spent the entire twenty minutes of the appointment concentrating on my breathing, desperate not to let the heat and the bright light of the small room make me puke all over it. I remember the midwife had a kind face and understood that it was a donor baby, yet everything else is a blur. She pointed at some dates and some phone numbers, gave me the file, told me I must always have it with me at every appointment, and then I sped out of the door and threw up in a bin amongst all the parked bikes outside. Another milestone that the sickness had robbed from me. Although, to be fair, I can't blame it all on the sickness, I have always struggled to listen when people are telling me important things.

I counted down the days to my twelve-week scan with excitement, not just because that would be when I would see my baby on screen for the first time, but because that is when everyone said the sickness would stop. That seemed like a fucking long time to wait to know if this little bean inside me was doing OK, though, so I booked to have an early 'viability' scan at a local private clinic. I felt a real need to placate the feelings I was having that this sickness meant that there was something wrong. It also seemed like a really good time to part with £120 . . .

My god, the clinic felt like a spa. It had a glass walkway floating over a flowing stream and The White Company toiletries. It felt like heaven – a world away from the dust and smell and chaos of my building-site home. Seconds after arriving I was taken to a huge room with a big medical bed in the middle and a desk to the side. The doctor explained that there was no time limit to my appointment and I could ask as many questions as I wanted. Of course, my mind was blank. I just wanted to know everything was OK. It seemed like such a small yet such a huge question at the same time.

So, with the formalities over, it was back to the familiar scene of me lying on a paper sheet, knickers off, legs apart, cold wand being moved around inside me. Woosh woosh woosh. The heartbeat. Everything was as it should be. The heartbeat was strong, all looked well and there was only one baby. I still don't know if I was relieved or sad about that. While I have no doubt it would have been bloody tough to have a multiple pregnancy, it would also have meant that the babies would always have had each other. I left feeling grateful and almost allowing myself to feel excited. Almost . . .

I was still staying with friends when I went to the hospital for my next scan – the legendary twelve-week one. I was desperate to see the miracle life that was growing inside me again. I was also pretty desperate for the nurse to press whatever button she needed to, to make the sickness go away. Because there had to be a way of making this stop, didn't there? Having finally found someone who would allow me to walk up the locked stairs of the hospital (I swear to god, the giant lift in that place actually swung from side to side like a pirate ship at a playground), I got to the reception with a flushed face and my blue folder. Again, everything went out of focus and I just ran back through the doors to find the loo. As that was obviously an occupational hazard, the pretty young woman sitting behind the desk didn't even bat an eyelid. She just sat flipping through my folder to find a barcode to scan me in.

I was, predictably, an hour early. The waiting room was a cluster of mixed emotions, the air heavy with anticipation. You could tell which women were there excitedly waiting for their first scan and which were nervously awaiting test results. Couples were silently holding hands, while others busily narrated the next steps. It was tropical in there, and every five minutes I had to take off another layer. I sipped my bottle of water, desperate to feel anything other than sickness. I just cannot explain the numb feeling that constant nausea gives you, you are blinkered to most things going on around you, other than planning the quickest route to the toilet, finding somewhere to lie down or windows to open. Stripped down to just a cotton dress and no shoes, I was finally called in to see the scan of my baby. Friends had offered to come with me for this momentous appointment, but I sort of felt like I needed to do this one alone. That it needed to be me and my baby.

What happened next was like an out-of-body experience. Things like this just didn't happen to me, yet I knew that in seconds I was going to see my baby on the screen for the second time. Inexplicably, this felt more legitimate to me than the private scan I had had over a month prior. Perhaps it was because this was the infamous Twelve Week scan that you would so often hear your friends talk about. Yet, I was never usually the person holding the strip of blurry black-and-white photos, but here I was, exposing my tummy so it could be smothered in cold, clear jelly and handing over a receipt to prove I had paid for the photographs to be printed. (I had just assumed you were given them, I didn't realise cold hard cash had to be exchanged. You see, I was a novice.) We lay in silence and then, crashing into the room, was THAT sound . . . the unmistakable rhythmic pulse of a heartbeat. Woosh, woosh, woosh. I was absolutely sure this was the moment I would break down and cry with relief, with excitement, with utter joy. Yet none of that happened, because I honestly, truly, could not believe this was happening to me. I know I keep saying it, but it is true, I was in a constant state of pure disbelief for months. The nurse and I spoke for a while and she pointed at various indistinguishable dots on the screen announcing their presence. Then she said the words, 'First of April.' My baby was due on April Fool's Day. Of bloody course it was, because this was still one big joke. I wasn't really going to have a baby. No way.

And yet, things seemed to be aligning at last. My house had finally been put back together, although the cost of the cowboy builder ate up the money I had put aside for maternity leave. I had wanted to take a good nine to twelve months to enjoy being with my baby, but now that wasn't a possibility – the money lost would also put me on financially rocky ground as soon as the baby was born. Yet I had a home, and it now had a full complement of walls and a roof, and I was so grateful to be back in it. On my turf. The smell of fresh building work, however, lingered throughout the house and would constantly ignite my sickness. I was still feeling nauseous, all day, every day. I could not believe I had made this happen to myself. I would wake up in the middle of the night, queasy. If I had to be sick, it was visceral. There were days when I could keep nothing down. People would tell me it was the sign of a strong baby, but my god, at that stage I would have been happy not to have had Anthony Joshua growing inside me.

Even though I couldn't keep much down, I still felt like eating, although I had no real cravings other than for Capri-Sun. I hadn't thought about those oddly shaped silver packets since my childhood, and I wasn't even sure if they still existed, then one night, around 2 a.m., I found myself driving to the nearest petrol station to quench my thirst. There was no Capri-Sun there. I remember being sick in a bag I found in the car and crying pathetic tears about the lack of that strong orange squash. The next day, I went on a mission to find the silver packets of orange nectar. Once I found them, I bought in bulk and solely kept that business alive for the next two months. I genuinely don't think I have ever had so much sugar in my life. Even now if I see one glinting at me in a petrol-station fridge, I have to buy it to sate my old cravings. I tried every old wives' tale under the sun to stop the sickness – the list went on and on, but nothing abated it. Sometimes the overwhelming feeling of it all made me so sad. I had wanted this so badly. I used to roll my eyes at pregnant people complaining of sickness. How bad can it be? Don't they know how lucky they are? Yet here I was growing a baby inside me like I had always hoped I would, and all I wanted was to not feel this way.

It is worth noting that if you are suffering from constant sickness and cannot keep food down, you should chat to your GP or midwife, so they can ensure you aren't getting dehydrated or give you the right treatment if you are. When it comes to your body and your pregnancy, always trust your gut, if things don't feel right, seek help.

I would wake in the middle of the night, sobbing alone into the still, silent air, terrified that I had made an appalling decision. If I couldn't cope with a little sickness, or the smell of a hotel lobby, then how on earth could I possibly look after a baby on my own? What wild arrogance had made me believe that I was capable of such huge and important responsibility?

THINGS THAT WILL 'APPARENTLY' HELP WITH MORNING SICKNESS, ACCORDING TO OLD WIVES

- Ginger
- Ginger biscuits
- Ginger sweets
- Try some ginger tea
- B6 at exactly the right time of the day

- Little meals often
- One big meal a day
- Don't eat at night
- Don't eat in the morning
- Snack in the night
- Travel sickness bands
- Avoid sugar
- Avoid fats
- Avoid peppers
- Avoid strong-smelling foods
- Avoid foods with flavour, except ginger, obvs
- Try aromatherapy
- Drink a lot of water
- Drink slowly
- Don't drink with meals
- Breathing

Those were the loneliest points. In the middle of the night, lying on my cold bathroom floor questioning my very existence and having no one there to talk me through it. The days and the nights at that point seemed so very, very long.

And yet, the times when I was not consumed by sickness, I was giddy with joy. I was having a bloody baby!

I had so much planned for us. It still felt unreal, like it wasn't something that was really happening to me. I had no bump, I had no partner, I had no nursery, I was constantly waiting for something awful to happen, for my joy to be whisked away. I didn't ever share the depth of my disbelief with anyone for fear that they would realise that it was true, I couldn't have a baby on my own. My body was making me doubt its own strength.

I knew that when I could find out the sex of the baby, I would be able to enjoy the ride much more. My sister came with me for the next scan, at eighteen weeks. This should have been my first inkling that pregnancies aren't nine months long, because they are only spoken about in weeks! Forty weeks does not make nine months. Even with a few five-week months thrown in for good measure, it is clear that forty weeks is nearer to ten months. Even if it wasn't, it sure as hell felt like it!

I was adamant I wanted a boy. I had absolutely no idea where this notion had come from or why, I just knew I had always pictured myself with a boy, so that is what I wanted this baby to be. Of course, all I really wanted was a healthy baby – that went without saying – it is just I wanted my healthy baby to be a healthy baby boy! My sister decided she should come with me because she knew if I found out it was a girl, I would need her to give me a strong talking to that I was being utterly ungrateful and bloody ridiculous by being upset about it.

When the sonographer asked if I wanted to find out the sex, my sister blurted out, with an anxious laugh, 'Depends what it is, she wants a boy.' The sonographer grinned widely and said, almost giggling, 'Good job, because this is a healthy little boy right here.' I started to breathe again; I had been holding my breath while my sister stroked my forehead like my mum used to. I quickly explained that I would have loved a girl too. We were both a bit teary and giddy. Relief washed over me. Not that I had found out I was having a boy, of course not, but because the fact he was no longer an 'it' made it feel actually, truly, really real. I was having a baby. I really was. A son.

A little later on in the pregnancy, I spoke to the doctor about the overbearing exhaustion and sickness – for a few weeks I was having around fifteen hours' sleep a night! The elusive twelve weeks had brought no respite from the tiredness and nausea, as everyone had promised. He wanted to make sure I didn't have gestational diabetes, so he sent me to have some tests. I am fine with having my blood taken, what I wasn't fine with was having to fast to do it, which was also necessary, apparently. The only thing that stopped me feeling like I was going to pass out was food. As soon as I woke up in the morning I needed to eat, even if it made me sick – that was better than the nausea that accompanied not eating. This blood test meant I couldn't eat for eight to ten hours before it was taken. Were they kidding? There was no way I could go that long without eating. I often had to wake in the night to sneak in a Mini Cheddar or two so I could go back to sleep. Ten hours with no food honestly seemed like a challenge too far.

I made sure the appointment was the first one they had available in the morning. I arrived feeling delirious with sickness, they took the test and then gave me a drink of glucose-y doom. Honestly, it was horrible. They then announced that I had to wait, in order to have another test two hours later, still having had no food. I was beside myself. I cannot adequately explain what this was like. It wasn't painful, but it was all-consuming. Every cell of my body was making me acutely aware that the hunger and the sickness were there. I lay on the floor of the huge reception area of my modern doctor's surgery, really concentrating on my breathing. I must have looked bonkers, or as if something terrible had happened. I honestly didn't care. I just wanted the feeling to go away, for them to take the test so I could neck a couple of Capri-Suns and some nuts.

The amazing nurse took my final blood test, stroked my forehead and offered me some water. I didn't want water, I wanted food! The automatic doors couldn't open fast enough and I went straight from the surgery to a coffee shop next door, tripping over myself, and ordered everything I could see on the menu. I had no idea what I wanted, but I wanted food and I wanted it quicker than they could possibly cook it! They brought out a bacon sandwich, granola, toast, a pain au chocolat, a fruit salad and some orange juice. I drank the juice, nibbled at the toast and didn't touch anything else. I drove home, stopping halfway to throw up, then as soon as I got through the door I got into bed and slept for twelve hours. This could not be normal. I had seen pregnant women at gyms, at nightclubs, at board meetings and none of them had to lie on the floor halfway through or puke in an office bin. What was wrong with me? Why wasn't I enjoying this? I so desperately wanted to enjoy this.

Once I knew I was having a boy and a bump started to form, I began to allow myself to believe that this was truly happening. The results of my diabetes test came back negative and my consultant at the hospital had said I was having a perfect pregnancy, 'under the circumstances'. For someone at the grand old age of thirty-eight with a high BMI daring to have a baby, I was doing OK. He informed me that I didn't need to be under consultant care anymore and he was more than happy for me to go to full term. If there was any risk to me or the baby, they may have had to see about having an induction earlier than forty weeks, but with neither me nor the baby showing any signs of any-thing untoward I was deemed 'passable' for a full-term pregnancy. He was very handsome, very handsome indeed, and I was glad I didn't have to go back to see him again, as I felt my face flush every time I sat opposite him! He still couldn't do anything about my sickness, though. I did ask. Repeatedly.

In my third trimester I decided to join an ante-natal class. From what I understood, these prepared you for birth and everything after, but all my friends seem to have done the course to meet other people having a baby at the same time as them, to create a midnight WhatsApp group demanding to know if anyone else's nipples felt like they were being bitten off. I knew that NCT was for couples, not just the pregnant person, and that it was pretty likely I would be the only single person there, but I decided to sign up anyway. I was excited to meet some people and find out more about labour, as I was relatively clueless about the whole giving birth bit of having a baby, and I couldn't work out if that was a bad thing or not.

Before you join the class, you have to fill out a lot of paperwork online. There was a tick box for who would be joining the group, so I ticked the small box next to 'Other' and explained there was no partner. A few days before the course started, the teacher called me to discuss 'my situation'. I immediately jumped to conclusions and assumed she would be asking me to go to another class of 'just women', or that single people couldn't join in at all. Of course she wasn't calling to say that, what was I thinking? She had, very sweetly, called to let me know that at the beginning of the class everyone is invited to introduce themselves and their partner, and she wanted to know if I would be comfortable with that or would I rather she made the introductions another way? It was such a kind thing to do, but I informed her that I was totally fine with explaining my situation.

Other than my usual awkwardness of walking into a room of strangers alone, I wasn't as anxious as I thought I might be when the first meeting came around. Having had the chat on the phone with the teacher beforehand, I was sort of prepared for what was coming. We shuffled some plastic chairs around the meeting space and everyone made awkward small talk. My eyes flicked round the room to try to spot the couples I knew I could make friends with. Some had laptops out ready to take notes, some were nervously making tea, some were looking deep into their partners' eyes so they didn't have to make conversation with strangers. Then our teacher started the class, asking us to introduce ourselves.

'Hello. I am Emma, this is Richard. We are due a little girl on the twenty-fifth of March. It is our first.'

'Hello, I am Richard and yes, we are due on twenty-fifth of March, this is our first but my second.'

And so on and so on, until it got to me. Very obviously sat on my own.

'Hey. I'm Liv. I am due a little boy on the first of April. I am single. It is a sperm donor baby. You can ask me any questions you like.'

There were definitely noises made. I am not sure what they were – perhaps shock, perhaps excitement, perhaps ambivalence, perhaps interest. I was just glad I had got it out of the way, the most awkward part was over. Well, that's what I had thought would be the most awkward part. Actually, the most awkward part turned out to be the fact that the course was designed for couples, so there were exercises for couples to do together. I, however, was left having to do them with the teacher. It screamed of not being picked for the school netball team. Butt-clenchingly embarrassing.

Week after week we joined together in a community hall and discussed what was just about to happen to our bodies, about the importance of birth plans to encourage a positive birth. We were shown various props that gave a visual representation of just how dilated we would become when we were in the full throes of labour. We were taught not to put a baby to sleep next to a radiator. We spent hours discussing breastfeeding. What different colours of poo meant. How to bathe the baby. The only thing that this course definitively taught me is that there are no answers. I sort of knew that, but every week this was really hammering it home. Every question asked by an anxious first-time mum, every opinion stated by one of the heavily pregnant women, was responded to with no definitive answers. Mainly because EVERYONE IS DIFFERENT and in many cases, you have limited control of what is going to happen.

MY BIRTH PLAN - CREATED WITH HINDSIGHT!

- Call the A Team.
- Get to hospital.
- Take all the drugs offered.
- No overhead lights, use battery-lit candles only, where possible. Overhead lighting is the destroyer of calm in any setting.
- Don't panic.

NB: This probably wouldn't be the birth plan advocated by birthing professionals!

I remember my chief learning was that I wasn't going to write a traditional birth plan (see above!). This is a very personal opinion, but through these meetings it sounded as though everything that I could wish for on the perfect birth plan could change at a moment's notice depending on how my baby and my body reacted to the situation. For me, the thought of writing detailed notes about hoping for a 'natural' birth in the calm of a mid-wife-led unit, having the ability to make good, informed choices for my baby and me, for that only to be dashed at a second's notice, when I would have felt at my most vulnerable, and then to be whizzed down to surgery, was a huge disparity that my mental health wouldn't cope with. I knew myself well enough to know that when plans do not work out, I can tailspin into panic. So my informed decision, that felt entirely right for me at that time, was to not have a formal birth plan. My birth plan consisted entirely of getting to the hospital, trusting the professionals and hoping they would give me drugs! I am notoriously a bit of a wuss, so it seemed that, for me, the chances were pretty high that I would need pain relief.

In psychology terms, this was probably the wrong way to go about thinking about The Pain. In fact, I had done a hypnobirthing course with my friend who was to become my birth partner, and we had discussed brilliant ways in which to reframe the narrative we have always been taught about the pain of childbirth into a more positive movement that was allowing you to get closer and closer to meeting your baby. I so wanted to believe this. I read a lot of books in my third trimester about this positive reframing of the birth experience, yet I knew that three months before the birth (which is when I started to seriously think about this) was not anywhere near enough time for my brain to rewire itself to make this a reality. I know it works, I have seen it work, I have heard the stories, but I wanted doctors and drugs. If I were to be lucky enough to have another child, I would be thinking differently, but with what I knew then, I knew I needed a plan that involved eliminating as many of the aspects that could possibly change.

Just when it felt like I was getting to grips with what was ahead of me, I missed a couple of the antenatal classes because my best friend of twenty-seven years was killed in a tragic accident. I was seven and a half months pregnant. She had a two-month-old baby and she was coming to my house to drop off some bits that he had grown out of and to hug my bump. I hadn't seen her since her second son had been born; two months go by pretty quickly when a month of it was over Christmas, and I was also giving her space to become accustomed to being a mum of two. She was late. She was never late. Ever. Or on the rare occasions she was, she would ring ahead and give you a specific new time of arrival. I was working from home and when I realised she was fifteen minutes late I texted her to let her know that I had a meeting a little later that I couldn't miss, so if it was easier we could make it another day. Not long after that I saw her mum's name come up on my phone. This wasn't unusual, I am very close to her family and I just assumed that she had told her mum that she was going to be late and that she was passing on the message.

'Hey, Mumma, are you being the messenger?'

'The worst thing has happened, my darling.'

I could tell in her voice that it was something really serious. She sounded vacant. I immediately thought about the baby. The baby I hadn't yet hugged.

'Oh my god, what is wrong with him, is he OK?'

'No darling, it is not the boys. She has gone.'

Flooded with relief that the boys were OK, I focused back on what she had just said.

'Gone where?'

Then I felt that feeling that I had been hiding since Mum died. It is so hard to describe. The world stops, you gasp for air, you know what you are hearing is true, yet you are in disbelief. You want to scream but you have nothing to give. I wanted to be with her mum so badly. I needed to smell her, to hold her. I knew I couldn't, it wasn't my place. I was home alone, seven and a half months pregnant, having just had the world kicked out from underneath me.

I am always waiting for tragedy, for the next awful thing to happen. When your childhood is ravaged by death and trauma, you always sleep with one eye open waiting for the next punch. Here it was, my Jen. She was the girl who drank with me when we pretended I was a DJ and she was an art student. She was the girl I phoned when I lost my virginity. She was the girl I watched *Wayne's World* with twenty times at the cinema. She was the girl I discovered music with. She was the girl whose mum would run me a bath when she realised it had all got too much at home when Mum was ill. She was the girl who held me when Mum died. She was the girl who we had a hen party for before her wedding, just me, her and her mum. She was the girl I watched walk down the aisle with her dad squeezing her hand. She was the girl who offered to help pay for my fertility treatment. She was the girl who studied so hard that she became a doctor. She was the girl who always, always, fluffed my feathers, sang my praises and made me feel golden. She was the girl who was going to be a godmother to my unborn son. She was gone.

I could not compute what was happening in my world. I had this glorious big belly which still seemed totally alien to me and I was talking to people about my Jen's funeral. My family rallied round me, as ever. When people die, everyone else shuffles closer together. This wasn't how my one pregnancy was supposed to be. I was supposed to feel glowing and alive, not sick and grieving. I only had the capacity to think about how it was affecting me. It was totally selfish. Yet the thought of her husband, sons, brothers and parents and their grief was too much for me to acknowledge. I wanted to be there for them and yet I knew I needed to keep my mental health in check for my baby. I had to do what I do best and put some form of barrier between my real raw emotions and the ones that I could allow myself to feel in that moment. I would wake in the night with that all-too-familiar pit of grief in my stomach, in combination with the 'morning' sickness that was still in full swing. I didn't know which was most prevalent, so I would just lie next to the toilet and weep until I needed to be sick again. Sometimes because of the grief, sometimes because of the pregnancy.

The weekend after Jen died, I was due to have my baby shower. Now, don't get me wrong, I usually barely tolerate such things, but this time, this time I had wanted it all! I hadn't had an engagement or a wedding or a honeymoon, so I wanted to dive head-first into celebrating my decision to go it alone. Also, and I am not going to sugar coat it, I needed stuff! Money was going to be tight and I didn't want people buying me cute things I didn't need. If they were going to kindly buy me anything I wanted it to be something practical or that I really, truly wanted. So, months before, I had put together a spreadsheet, sent it to my best friends and asked (OK, fine, I told them!) to organise me something lovely! It was something I was really looking forward to. A celebration.

When Jen died, I could not contemplate celebrating my baby less than a week later. Everyone was so kind and understanding and happy to abide by whatever decision I made about whether or not it should go ahead. My head was numb, I couldn't think straight. I decided to think about what Jen would do in this situation. She was a clinical psychologist, so she would have had ways to process all this much better than I was seeming to. I realised there was no right or wrong answer. My Jen wasn't going to come back if I decided to cancel that lunch. What the baby shower was going to do, though, was allow me to be surrounded by people I loved and that was actually exactly what I needed at that moment.

So we went ahead as planned. A really low-key lunch at a great pub, with all my family and friends – with one even flying in from Geneva. A photo of Jen with her sparkling eyes and beaming smile was set next to a glowing candle. The irony is that she would have hated that day! She would have liked to have seen everyone, even though she didn't know many of them as they were friends I had collected over the years, and she was a stalwart, but I know she would have felt anxious about attending. Nothing a little blast of Lionel Richie wouldn't have sorted out, though.

The warmth that enveloped me that day from everyone was overwhelming, I will never forget it. I couldn't make this better, I couldn't fix this, I had to learn to live this new life without her and ensure I looked after myself for the final few weeks of my pregnancy. That is exactly what she would have wanted. A couple of days later, her hero of a husband dropped off the gifts Jen had bought for me from the spreadsheet I had created. I had wanted practical presents because that is what I needed, but not now. Not from Jen. So I took the bag to the baby shop she had bought them from to try to exchange the practical gifts I had requested for sentimental ones I felt I needed instead. I didn't have the receipt, so I just blurted out what had happened to the girl behind the counter, me and my glorious belly shaking with tears. She rushed over to hug me and told me I could exchange anything at all, no problem. So back went the babygrows and changing mat, and in their place we gained a very traditional teddy bear that has sat inside my boy's cot ever since. From his godmother he never met, always near.

As I approached eight months, I couldn't tell if the sickness was abating slightly or I was just used to it after all this time. I couldn't distinguish the lines between grief and exhaustion either. What I did know was that this baby was imminent and my abs had never felt so hard! Some women, understandably, don't like it when strangers touch their bumps, I, on the other hand, actively encouraged it. Having spent my entire adult life hiding my stomach through inexplicable shame, I was now happy to show it off at any opportunity. The fragile little life growing and kicking inside me was giving my body the most magnificent form and I was loving every second of talking to it, stroking it, telling him stories about Jen, playing him my favourite tunes, telling him about his grandparents, lovingly massaging oil into my skin. I think I was finally, finally accepting that this was actually happening. I really was going to have a baby.

My craving for Capri-Sun had been replaced with a healthier one for oranges, and these sensations were so intense by this stage that Jen's brother was delivering me brown paper bags overflowing with sweet blood oranges every two or three days. At one stage

I was on about fifteen a day. Can you imagine?! You know the old adage, 'you are what you eat'? Well, that was becoming more and more true. I was as round as I was tall, and with the fake tan I was liberally applying to try to make me look 'well', I could easily have been going to a fancy dress party as an orange with no costume at all. I was sniffing wild orange essential oils while simultaneously eating way more than I actually needed, but definitely as much as my body wanted. The sweet citrus aroma would stop my senses from wanting to be sick, because even at the very latter stages of pregnancy my morning sickness was in full swing. Of my whole pregnancy there were two weeks, at around the thirty-week mark, that I felt good. Just two weeks. I was so desperately sad for myself, that the cute fairytale pregnancy I had written in my head was the very opposite of my reality! All I had done throughout this time was whinge, and yet I knew how very bloody lucky I was. My body may well have felt like someone else's but my mind was very present.

I was so impatiently excited to meet my boy. When you don't know what 50 per cent of the DNA of your unborn child is, you constantly wonder what they will look like. Will you recognise them? Will they look nothing like you? While what a baby looks like is absolutely not important, the fact that you will have no clue what they *might* look like is quite an odd feeling. My whole body was tingling with anticipation as the forty-week finish line came ever nearer. When the time came for my thirty-six-week scan (which is not routine in some healthcare trusts, but it was in mine) I was wild with excitement about the fact I may be able to see him 'properly'. I hadn't seen his pixelated little body for over four months and back then he didn't even have a name. By this stage I was very much his mum and even though he punched me all the time, I felt like he loved me too. So the thought of actually seeing him on the screen was a day I was longing for just as much as the birth itself. I lay on the bed and got into the usual position, exposing my magnificent belly that had a pearlescent shine to it due to the skin being stretched so much. The familiar rhythmic sound filled the room and I twisted my head impatiently to get a good look at him. Bugger. Bugger. Bugger. Turns out he still just looked like a pixelated version of a baby. Any baby. I remember being so gutted that I would have to really, truly wait until his birth day before I could get a glimpse of the life I had created.

Having taken the usual measurements, I was told that at thirty-six weeks he weighed around 7lb 7oz.

Woah! Babies grow around half a pound a week from that point on, so if I went to full term, it was looking like I was going to have a nine-pounder – at least! While the prospect of a big baby working his way through my body was pretty daunting, I was thrilled at the thought of the chubby little babe coming out the other side. Nothing cuter than a babe, all thigh rolls and big cheeks. I fantasised about clutching those chubby little rolls of sweet-smelling baby skin and kissing his rounded cheeks.

For now, though, I just had to wait. I could go into labour at any point. This felt like torture. My whole body was cloaked in every emotion I could think of; fear, excitement, angst, joy, grief, astonishment and impatience were dominating my every waking thought. The worst part was there was no deadline. It was like the stomach-churning excitement you have on Christmas Eve when you are a child, yet you never knew when Christmas Day was going to be. As each day passed, this bubbling excitement dissipated more and more until it became impatience.

I was bursting at the seams in the most beautiful way, both physically and mentally. My due date was 1 April, which this year was Easter Sunday. I bloody love Easter, it is like Christmas, but without the stress.

I usually host a big lunch for friends and go overboard with unnecessary decorations and a table groaning with food piled onto it. Obviously, this time I passed the baton and danced around someone else's living room with bunny ears on, still secretly convinced that any minute now a noisy theatrical pop of my waters breaking would fill the room. I loved the thought of him arriving at Easter; a time of year full of blossom, birdsong and, let's be honest, hot cross buns. I lovingly rubbed my belly, knowing it wouldn't be around much longer in its current abundant, rock-solid form. We had an Easter-egg hunt, we ate lamb, we danced, I threw up, we all hugged excitedly, assuming this would be the last time they saw me pregnant and then I drove home. The bunny ears came off, the sun set and yet there was no sign of the boy. The April Fool's due date was starting to feel like a distant memory. The joke really was on me.

CHAPTER 5: FORTY PLUS FOURTEEN

This whole chapter is about giving birth. I totally get it if that isn't your thing, and if so, you can skip on by to page 218.

Spoiler: I gave birth.

The due day came and went. I drove over speed bumps as fast as was allowed. I ate pineapple three times a day. I was sipping raspberry leaf tea like my life depended on it. Curries were consumed at an alarming rate. I tried every old wives' tale going. Except sex, obviously! Yet nothing happened. Phone calls, texts, DMs of people desperate for news, as if I had had the baby and just forgot to tell them. 'Oh, the baby? Yeah, I had him last week, didn't I say?'

Having spoken to a few people who have also gone overdue, it is my firm belief that some witchcraft happens in those days to make you totally, utterly and deeply lose the plot. I had been sorting out the house for the last three months ready for my baby's birth – my niece had painted my bedroom, my nephew had sorted the garden, my brother-in-law had assembled my £10 Facebook marketplace cot, I had filled skips with junk, had the dog groomed, stuffed the freezer with meals, packed my hospital bags with various shit I didn't need and I had made sure his bedroom was 'perfect', ready for him. I had never been so prepared for anything. WHERE. THE. FUCK. WAS. HE? I was seriously lucky in the fact that I slept well (bar the sickness) throughout my pregnancy, with the aid of the greatest pregnancy pillow of all time and my innate need to be asleep as often as possible. Apart from a brief spell of insomnia after Mum died, I have always been a cracking sleeper. I got the good nocturnal genes from my dad, as well as the rugby thighs, hairy face and appalling temper, so, you know, fair is fair! I cannot imagine how irrational I would have been had I not been sleeping during that time, but it's fair to say my friends and family are seriously grateful that I was.

The days dragged and dragged as I waited for signs of labour. Did my left toe just tingle? Is that a sign? I was convinced farts were contractions. I had eaten all the snacks in my hospital bag at least twice. I tried to check my vagina hadn't in fact closed up and the baby just couldn't physically get out. Every morning I woke fizzing with excitement that today was going to be The Day I Met My Son. Yet each evening I would still be sitting on the sofa, eating more replenished snacks, livid. Was I going to die at eighty-seven, still pregnant? Elvis, who had always taken a shine to pregnant women, could not get close enough to me; I felt like an odd marsupial hybrid who had a child inside not wanting to come out and a child outside desperate to get in. We went for long walks in the meadow to try to encourage the baby to come and meet us and I continued to work my way through the list of every old wives' tale ever told. Forty plus six, and nothing.

That's another thing no one tells you about pregnancy, that all usual formats of time go out of the window. When you become pregnant, the only month that is ever spoken of is month nine, and THAT DOESN'T EVEN EXIST. Doing the four times table on my fingers was a common occurrence when it was demanded of me to know how many weeks pregnant I was. This also coincided with comparing the size of my foetus to various fruits. Week six it was a pomegranate seed, week twenty-two a spaghetti squash, week thirty-five a honeydew melon. I couldn't even spot a spaghetti squash in a supermarket line up, let alone be able to relate its size to the living creature writhing around inside me. Then, out of nowhere, you reach forty weeks, the holy grail, the due day and suddenly no one speaks about weeks anymore. It is weeks and days now. No one tells you this, it just happens. You are asked by the medical staff how far gone you are and I would say, 'Oh full term, forty weeks.'

'Exactly forty weeks?'

'Well and a couple of days.'

'How many days? When was your due date?'

Every day beyond my due date felt like an eternity and I was expected to know how many of these days had gone by and add that on to a weekly metric of time that felt like it had passed at least four months ago.

'April Fool's Day, first of April.'

'Ah, OK, you are forty plus four, you should come in for a check-up.'

So my forty-week plus four-day bump waddled, literally waddled, into the doctor's surgery, after I'd thrown up in the bin outside for old times' sake. I think this was about the time they started talking about 'having a sweep'. This is a procedure that involves fingers, hopefully those of a midwife, rummaging around your cervix in order to try to stimulate the hormones that encourage labour.

Or something like that. All I knew was that I wasn't up for it. Despite the fact I would have given nearly all the crisps I owned to get this baby out of my belly and into my arms, there was no guarantee that the sweep was definitely going to make that happen. It might encourage labour, but not definitely. At this point, this sort of medical fingering needed to have a definitive result for me to agree to it. Unless it was going to make that baby slide out of my vagina like a well-oiled penguin on a slide, I wasn't going to have any fingers fiddling around up there, thank you.

TOP TIPS FOR CHOOSING YOUR A TEAM

- Ask your friends/family if they want to be your birthing partner, but be mindful of sensitivities and don't assume everyone will think it is a great privilege.
- You need someone/people who will be able to drop everything at an undisclosed time and date, even if that is the middle of the night.
- Pick someone/people who is/are as happy to hold your hand as well as tell you to pull yourself together.

- Ensure your partner/s know your wishes in the event of an emergency, don't leave them in the tricky position of having to make assumptions if the worst should happen.
- You need to make sure you feel really comfortable with your chosen few – like, they may see you shit yourself and your vagina explode type of comfortable.
- Most importantly, pick people who won't post photos of you in the throes of labour on a group WhatsApp/social media site.

The other people waiting nearly as impatiently as me for my body to kick into action were my birthing partners. Yes, there were multiple. I have always worked in excess, so why stop at one birthing partner when I can have three? It is a tricky thing to choose who will be with you when you are at your most vulnerable, most excited, most scared – and most naked! Especially when none of those people are responsible for you being in that state. Usually, there is some degree of flexibility for the partner of the pregnant person in terms of their usual daily routine, like work. However, this is more difficult to swing when you need unplanned time off to help your friend in labour. So I threw a text out to my nearest and dearest (girls only, although I would have loved to have seen what excuses my male mates would have given to not be available, or, worse, which would have agreed to do it!) to ask if anyone in fact *wanted* to be there. You can't just assume people will be thrilled that you asked them. It may be their worst nightmare. Committing to a date that wasn't exact when people had lives of their own was tricky. Also, as my baby was due in the Easter holidays, loads of people had already booked to go away. Some could do Tuesdays and Wednesdays between 4 p.m. and 7.30 p.m., if it wasn't the fourth Wednesday of the month when it was their turn for the Brownie pick-up. Or they would absolutely love to hold my hand, unless it was 6 April, as that was their mum's birthday.

Selfishly, my need for as much control in an out-of-control situation as possible meant that unless people could commit 100 per cent to be flexible and available, I just couldn't accept their offer of dealing with me in labour! Two people I knew who couldn't say no were my poor, ever-supportive, ever-loving sisters. Although one of them, who would literally turn her life upside down for me, would not forfeit the skiing holiday she had planned! Outrageous! So we had to make a contingency plan in case she wasn't here, because leaving it up to just one sister seemed a bit mean. One of my best mates was also due to be on holiday, so she wasn't a definite either. Imagine booking a holiday when your sister/best mate could be going into labour? Wildly selfish, if you ask me! Then there was brilliant Claire, who was in control of her own time, lived close by and has an amazing mum who could and would (happily!) scoop up Claire's three boys even if it was in the middle of the night, if that was what was needed. Bingo! I now had one sister who had tirelessly arranged for staff to run her deli so she could whizz up to Oxford at the drop of a hat, a definite in Claire, and two galavanting possibles depending on which one was in the country when the big arrival took place. All bases covered! I wouldn't be on my own and they wouldn't be on their own with me. Even Elvis had his own plan of action in the form of our ace neighbour and a close friend who were to share the dog-sitting duties. He loves both of them more than me, and they were both ready to have him for as long as necessary and could just let themselves in and whisk him away. So, he was one thing off my list of things to worry about.

And yet, still the baby didn't come. Farts were still farts and not contractions, I was on at least round five of the hospital snacks and my sense of humour had

evaporated days before forty plus six. Forty plus nine
. . . Forty plus eleven. On and on the days went. On
and on and on. This whole pregnancy was a brilliant
peek into the future of never being in control of my
life again! It was just one long, exciting slide down
into the pool of parenthood, where once in you have
to dive to the bottom to find your life jacket, but you
aren't sure if you can swim underwater just yet.

It was at about this stage that it looked more and more
likely that I would need to have an induction. Depending on your personal preference and your healthcare
trust in England, it is uncommon to be encouraged to
have a pregnancy go past forty plus fourteen. If your
baby is showing no signs of making their own way
out, then that is the time they would often be helped
along by way of an induction. As with everything pregnancy related, there are a million caveats to this, but
this is a finger-in-the-air, general rule of thumb for my
healthcare trust. I am sure it is based on more than a
finger-in-the-air guess, but you know what I mean.

The upshot of this was that my labour was going
to be started artificially by way of gel in the vagina.
Yet more glamour. If ever I spoke about induction to
people, they would do that sucking air motion that
builders express when they are just about to give you

a quote. With a sort of sorrowful look in their eyes. Rarely did anyone say anything comforting. I hadn't even looked into whether I might want my pregnancy to go on longer than forty plus fourteen, if I am honest, as I had always presumed I would go into labour naturally while walking through a meadow as the sun set around me, and the passing birds would airlift me to the delivery suite. At this stage, I was so wrapped up in emotions of overwhelm and excitement that the very thought that my pregnancy might go on longer than that of the average elephant was unimaginable. Bearing in mind that by now, based on my thirty-six-week scan measurements, the baby inside me was well over ten pounds. My vagina couldn't cope with a speculum let alone this apparently gargantuan baby. So I ignored all the empathetic smiles, listened to the pros and cons of induced labour (I mean, when I say I listened, I don't remember a word of what they said, as ever, so I can't promise I did) and hastily agreed.

I was told someone from the midwifery team would call to tell me when I should come into the hospital to start the induction process. My birth team (I am not sure the term 'birth partner' is relevant when there are three of them) were warned, bags were packed, tenterhooks were out and snacks replenished, again.

Obviously, you can't just dictate when you can go in, you have to be told when beds will be free and at the weekend this would sometimes take a little longer. This was, of course, the weekend. Still no call. FOR THE LOVE OF MARMITE WILL SOMEONE GET THIS BABY OUT OF ME! I needed to meet him, I needed to not feel sick, I needed to know what labour was going to be like, I needed to know that he and I would both get through it OK, I needed the fucking nervous anticipation that had been bubbling up for over six weeks – or even thirty years – to stop. What had also dawned on me around this time was that my late dad's birthday was fast approaching. Imagine if my boy was born on his grandad's birthday? It had never even entered my conscience that this could even be a possibility, as Dad's birthday was sixteen days after my due date. Sixteen days. There was no way I was going to be pregnant that long, they wouldn't allow it, surely? I just wanted to meet my boy.

The call came. Finally, the call came. I was to go in the next morning at eight. Holy bananas! It was happening. Definitely, really happening. In thirty-six hours' time, I would have a baby. I started to clean the house, change the sheets, cook a lasagne, reorganise his babygrows that would never, ever be organised again and shave my legs, well, the parts I could reach. OK, so I shaved my toes. Sure, the rest of my body was like a Barnum act, but thank god I would have hairless toes. My sister had her deli being looked after, my other sister had returned from holiday and Claire was chomping at the bit to come and collect me. I got into my freshly made bed and felt a sense of extraordinary relief wash over me. It was finally going to be Christmas tomorrow. I set my alarm and fell asleep.

THINGS I TOOK TO HOSPITAL IN MY MASSIVELY OVERPACKED BAG THAT I ACTUALLY USED:

- Battery operated candles.
- My own pillow.
- Two enormous cotton nighties.
- Caudalie Beauty Elixir.
- Hair bands.
- Arnica tablets.
- Socks.
- Change for the outrageously expensive car park which still only took cash.
- TENA pants. It wasn't just my baby who left the hospital in a nappy.

It felt like 3 a.m. when my alarm went at 7 a.m., my body frenzied with both hope and fear. I was reminded of being woken in the middle of the night by my dad when we had to catch a plane in the early hours for a holiday, my body cold, numb and unusually alert. I whizzed around the house, making sure I had everything. By everything, I mean everything. I needed Sherpas; I had a hospital bag, the baby had a hospital bag, there was a bag of 'things to do', my pillow, my pregnancy pillow of dreams and the bountiful snack bag. Claire arrived, a mum of three who knew the landscape of what was about to happen far better than I did, animated yet inherently calming. We filled her car with the plethora of crap I was taking that I wouldn't need, snapped our seatbelts into position and started the two-mile journey to the hospital.

I don't need to point out that those two miles were epic, like a scene from the Nevada Desert, where the hospital was a mere mirage in the distance. When we at last got there all of five minutes later, we were shown into the room. It was palatial! I had asked for somewhere with windows, if possible, as the thought of having no natural light for hours was something I really wanted to avoid, I didn't want to feel like I was in an airless vortex. There was a bed for me, a bed for one of my team, a bathroom, kettle, microwave, armchair . . . the lot! Honestly, I had imagined giving birth in a tiny room made out of a corridor like the one I was in when I got pregnant all those months before.

The midwife came in and explained what was going to happen, as I whipped off my pants and got into position for yet another internal rummage by someone I had known for less than ten minutes. It was while this was happening that somehow we realised that she was in fact the wife of the dreamy builder who had come to patch up the shit work of the cowboy. I am sure I have had more surreal moments, but I can't remember when.

Then Claire and I sat and waited. I had kind of assumed that as soon as I had had the induction gel applied, my waters would erupt, my contractions would start and within a couple of hours I would be holding my boy. I was getting anxious that my sisters hadn't arrived yet. Of course they hadn't, they were mothers of three and knew how long this could take. Another lesson in never being in control again. What happened over the subsequent forty hours is a slight blur. My sisters arrived, the lasagne I had cooked the day before made its way to the hospital, along with roughly 6,576,538 battery operated tealights, you know, for a little ambience as you prepare for your world to be flipped upside down via a ten-pound baby travelling through your body to reach the other side. In fact, my waters were broken for me, so there was no sensational waterfall in Waitrose as I had once hoped, meaning I would be in receipt of a year's free groceries, or so the legend goes.

My contractions started without fanfare. They just sort of came. This time it wasn't a fart. The pain was bearable at first and our little gang slowly lost their minds over rounds of charades. Eventually night fell and the light of the plastic candles created a vague atmosphere of calm in a room full of impatience. Each team member took it in turns to sleep on the pull-out bed and the chair as I drifted in and out of sleep and discomfort. We waited for a room in the delivery suite to become free. I think we were on our third midwife shift by this point as she came in to tell me that they were ready for me. Oh. My. Christ. Here we go.

We packed up the detritus I had brought with me and meandered through the hospital in the small, eerily quiet hours of the early morning. I made the whole team come down the stairs with me, as now was not the time for me to get stuck in that antique lift. We reached the depths of the hospital and my stretched tummy was aching heavily. Our delivery room wasn't quite as luxurious as the candlelit, micro-wave-laden living room we had lucked out with upstairs, and there was no spare bed (not that I was expecting one!). Instead, there was a selection of vast beanbags flopped in the corner. Another midwife appeared, taking everything in her stride, full of Irish charm and just a touch of 'buckle up, you've got this'. I was offered an epidural – and I couldn't have agreed to it faster. Oddly, or perhaps not, the epidural (which is entirely voluntary and scenario-dependent) was the only part of labour that I was truly fearful about. I knew the benefits were likely to outweigh the fact that a large needle was being placed into my spine and the consequences that may bring. A needle into my spine. Needle. Spine. Not a good thought, but my inability to manage my pain with just the gas and air that I was merrily inhaling cancelled out my fear.

A doctor came in with an eager student sidekick. My team left as everyone decided them being there might be a distraction and, for obvious reasons, I needed to keep calm and still. I was anything but calm: I was hungry and tired and my emotions were spiralling out of control. I sat on the edge of the bed, crying, as a man rooted around my spine. After a little while he turned to the student next to him and declared, too loudly, that they were going to need a bigger needle. You had got to be kidding me. I wanted everything to stop. The pain. The harsh blue light of the room. The exhaustion. The fear. The whole having a baby thing. What the fuck had I done? I wanted it all to stop.

I vividly remember the face of that man as he apologised for it being a 'difficult one' and left the room with a spring in his step, leaving me with my legs dangling over the edge of the high bed like a vulnerable child. Things got more intense pretty quickly from that point. I was heavily invested in my relationship with the gas and air and every time my sister tried to manage my intake of it, I snarled at her to return it to where it belonged immediately. As far as I was concerned, it belonged with me, at all times. I was agitatedly trying to remember the counting I should do, as instructed in the hypnobirthing course. Ironically, anything happening in an agitated manner is pretty much the opposite of everything you are taught with hypnobirthing, so the fact that I thought this might help was a loss from the start. I couldn't remember if I was supposed to breathe in for longer, or for the exhale to be the long one. Did I have to hold my breath? I started to count, apparently in no particular order, and whenever one of the team tried to steer me on to the right track of basic counting I would hiss and huff and continue . . . 6, 4, 9, 10 . . . comically clinging on to my desperation to be in control.

My sisters took turns to stroke my forehead as Mum would have done, trying in vain to get me to regain any composure I could muster. The pain began to spike and I couldn't believe that I had hyped myself up to get an epidural for it to have not made any real difference. Turns out the epidural had fallen out. The bloody needle had fallen out. I couldn't believe it. I felt like a deflating balloon, all-flailing lack of control and burst excitement. I could tell that everything was taking its toll on the team, too; Claire was not sure how to help, one sister was weeping in the corner and the other was trying to calmly but forcefully tell me to get my shit together. Me losing control was not going to help anyone. Especially not this tiny baby.

An amazing anaesthetist came in to offer another epidural. I almost spat out my words of refusal, so vehement was I that I wasn't going to go through that again. Yet I had no energy to fight the pain and I just wanted it to go away. Eventually she persuaded me and the epidural went in with no fuss, no pain, no demands for extra-long needles. I was thrilled. I suspect it was the drugs, but just her manner had made the process feel much more personal and less intimidating.

I had been told I couldn't eat in case I had to have surgery, but I hadn't eaten for nearly a day by now, and I was so hungry. I was offered a cup of tea, which I demanded to have with sugar – against all advice. I promptly threw that up and pathetically agreed to just be hungry. Then the door opened and the hot consultant walked in. The one who had told me that he was happy for me to go full term because I was having a perfectly healthy pregnancy. I wanted to scream at him for allowing this to happen, for allowing me to have a perfectly healthy pregnancy, which in turn meant I could get to the stage of needing to be induced. Of course, it wasn't his fault, and me trying to claim so was obviously something he was used to, as he just grinned and told me to basically stop all my ridiculous antics and concentrate on getting the job done!

It was exactly what I needed to hear, with my mind and body tangled in exhaustion and determination. I knew there was talk of surgery at this stage, although no one was saying it to me yet. A beautiful, terrifyingly young doctor came in and explained to me that the baby's head was out but the rest of the body wasn't coming through, so they would likely need to take me to the theatre to try to help him out with forceps. To physically pull him out of my body. I have no doubt she used less brutal language, but I knew what she meant; her colleagues were going to attach some archaic-looking apparatus around my unborn baby's head and forcibly pull him out, like when a pair of wellies get a vacuum inside them and you need a friend to heave them away from your foot, then you watch as the release propels them across the room in a heap. Except this wasn't a welly and a foot. This was my son and my vagina.

All we had to do now was wait for a theatre to become available. Just wait. It felt extraordinary, almost as if I was watching from afar, yet I knew I could feel the pain despite my delirium. The room seemed manic and crowded at this point, I was pathetic and almost lifeless, my arms flailing to the side of me, and I didn't even have the gumption to suck at the gas and air without someone else holding it for me. Every time someone came into the room, I demanded to know if the theatre was ready yet, I tried to make jokes – I didn't feel funny, it is just my natural reaction to anything I am uncomfortable with. I begged for help, and I know I used the word barbaric on more than one occasion. I was so worried about my baby, yet simultaneously I wanted to just give up. The delivery suite at this stage was loaded with frenzied emotion. My team were desperate to alleviate my fears, my pains and to try to calm me, but they too were exhausted and anxious.

Eventually I was told my time had come to go to theatre, for my son to be born, for this distress – both his and mine – to end. I was briefed about what would happen should they not be able to birth him with the aid of forceps. I was advised that as his head was already delivered, that in order for him to come out safely they would need to basically pull his head back through my vagina for him to be birthed via caesarean section. BACK THROUGH MY VAGINA? I had never heard of anything like that before and yet I remember that my overriding feeling at that stage wasn't fear, it was relief that this was all going to be over soon. Surely?

Only one of my loyal and battered team was allowed into theatre with me. It felt so shit that they had all battled through with me this whole time and yet they weren't going to be there for his 'glorious' arrival. My sister, Annie, is innately caring and yet, as a physiotherapist, deals with difficult people all the time, so she knows how to be compassionate with a healthy side order of 'suck it up'. Perhaps not the level of difficult I was producing, but still, I knew she would hold my hand while being stern enough to not let me spiral into a panic that would be irreversible. I was wheeled out of the delivery suite at pace, leaving behind my other sister and Claire with tears and concern in their eyes. Annie held my hand. The intense light of the theatre was almost ferocious. The room was filled with a cacophony of clattering and hushing and talking and whizzing round while I just lay there, helpless and desperate. Everyone in that room – the surgical team, the anaesthetist, the midwives, the nurses, the paediatric consultant – each and every one introduced themselves to me and explained their role in what was about to happen. While it was comforting to know they were real human people who would do everything they could to keep my baby and me safe, all I wanted them to do was shut up and get him out.

The only name I remembered was that of the anaesthetist. In the same way that you should always make friends with the bar staff at a wedding so they keep you topped up, I figured I should try to become friends with the guy with the painkillers so he could MAKE THIS STOP. I kept saying his name, over and over and over again. The poor guy, being pleaded with by a geriatric pregnant lady, pathetically thrashing around on the hospital bed begging for him to give her the good stuff. As if he had any other option. My poor sister was trying to calm me, while continuing to stroke my head and offer reassurance. Then, at last, the intensity of the pain just went away. I could just see two heads bobbing around over the dividing curtain they had placed between the top and bottom halves of my body. My eyes were barely open; I wanted to know what was happening.

Through this whole process, I had explained to every single medical professional, literally all 42,345 of them, that it was my dead dad's birthday today and the only reason all this would be worth going through would be to have my son born on that day. So I was adding pressure on pressure. Of course, no one could do anything about the timing of things, but at 11.30 p.m. it looked very unlikely that that particular cherry was going to adorn this cake. The buzz of the room continued, noises everywhere. Beeping from machines, talking amongst colleagues, calming reassurance from my sister, clattering from surgical instruments, and then suddenly my sister excitedly proclaimed his arrival. I saw them lift him over the curtain through my one open eye, and then they whisked him off. There had been no cry. I had watched enough episodes of *One*

Born Every Minute to know that no cry isn't ideal. The chattering stopped, but the various machines carried on their overture.

It almost felt too quiet, though, and still there was no cry. I lay, exhausted, with my son out of my sight, terrified, yet without any energy to give in to the acute anxiety in my head. Then, suddenly, a pathetic but very real little cry came from behind me and the noise picked up again. It was 11.50 p.m. on my dad's birthday. I had done it. We had done it. We were all safe and well.

They bundled him up and handed him to my sister, who knew that the baby she was handing me was not the bouncing bundle of round-cheeked 10lb baby-boy that I had been anticipating. She had tears in her eyes and the most comforting of smiles on her face and as she handed him to me, she was not surprised by my, 'Is that one mine? It looks like E.T.!'

I think I had thought he was going to come out looking like some sort of baby from a Boden catalogue, and instead I was lying there like an upturned tortoise being handed a long, thin, bruised, skinned rabbit. 'Yes, darling, that is your son,' she reassured me confidently.

She laid him on me and I tried to hug him, nuzzle him, look at him, but my swollen boobs, each the size of a small melon, were wobbling up towards my chin, so the poor baby didn't really have anywhere to go! They took him away again to clean him up and weigh him while I was stitched up, thankfully still unable to feel a thing. I was so thrilled to hear he was healthy and safe, but I just wanted to go home to bed. I had assumed that once the pain had stopped, I would be enveloped by a comforting feeling of love, pleasure and joy. Yet I was empty, I had barely anything to give. Just as I closed my eyes in the hope of sleep and respite, a kind-faced man put his hand on my shoulder and explained to me that I was not to worry but the baby had quite a lot of bruising to his face, and his head was a little misshapen due to the forceps delivery. *Oh, cool, that explains the contorted, skinned rabbit look.*

While I shouldn't have to point out that of course I didn't *actually* care what my son looked like, it felt wild not to know what he *could* look like because I was totally blinkered to one half of his genetics. So when the idyllic (and basically absurd!), bouncing, rosy-cheeked 10lb baby I had conjured up in my head turned out to actually be a squashed, skinny, 7lb, almost grey, wailing banshee, I couldn't help but feel something akin to shock. While this was going on, to my left my sister had passed out! The heat, the procedure, the anxiety, the lack of sleep had all caught up with her and she was bundled onto a seat and was being cared for by one of the amazing nurses. Honestly, if it hadn't all been so fraught it would have been bloody comical.

It was an odd feeling at that point. Piled on top of the exhaustion was something I can only think of as a feeling of failure. While I had deliberately not concocted a strict birth plan that would have had to go out of the window, I had somehow assumed that I would at least have been able to deliver my own baby. Yet the little skinned rabbit had to be coerced out of his warm, watery burrow with brute force and steel apparatus because I had failed to push him out sufficiently.

I had also planned on having my placenta made into pills. If you had told me I was going to be 'that mum' when I was in my twenties, I would've spat out my Marlboro Light. Yet here I was, having paid someone to come and collect my placenta in a carefully labelled, sterilised Tupperware box that I had bought especially (choosing the size took hours, I mean, what size is a placenta? I just assumed it was enormous) in order for it to be freeze-dried and returned to me as pills. I had read that it could help with the reduction in postpartum mood disorders as well as increase energy levels, so I thought it couldn't possibly hurt to try. Anything for a good mood and high energy if gin was off the cards! However, there are strict guidelines about the health of the placenta meeting a certain level for it to be encapsulated – somewhat obviously. Guess what? I no longer matched the criteria. Of course I didn't! I can't even remember what it was that had happened for it to no longer be viable, meconium possibly, I just have visions of a nurse waving around what looked like a large bloody liver and shaking her head.

So, the pregnancy had been shit (not dreadful, but definitely not blooming), I hadn't managed to birth my own son, I hadn't eaten for what felt like twenty years, I was off my face on drugs and exhaustion, I couldn't have my placenta turned into energy elixir, I had given birth to a skinned rabbit rather than a chubby, red-cheeked Viking, two doctors were still fiddling around in between my legs cleaning and stitching me up like a well-worn jumper ready to be used again, my sister had passed out and I could no longer feel my legs. Have a baby, they said.

I was wheeled out of the frenzied white light of the theatre to a hushed half-dark ward. It was now the early hours of the morning, so the hospital was bathed in an eerily still calm, which felt like such sweet reprieve. Claire and Sally were waiting and they each held the baby while gently weeping with content relief. I had no feeling from my tummy down, so I was still just lying flat on the bed, hoping for sleep to wash over me. Then suddenly a nurse appeared and she started talking about feeding the baby. The next thing I knew, he was forcefully shoved at my mountainous boob under the bedside light. I suspect he felt suffocated and he quickly retreated from the warm milk buffet I was proffering. Another rejection. Suddenly nurses' hands, my sisters' hands, probably a couple of passers-by, too, it felt like at that stage, were all trying to get this fragile mini body to latch on to my nipple that was escaping down towards my armpit as I couldn't sit up to get into a position that would have suited us both. He and I were weary from our ordeal and I don't know if I asked it to stop, or they all decided to stop, but suddenly everyone was saying their goodbyes to me.

My glorious team were leaving my side for the first time in over two days. There were tears and kisses and strokes of love – and then they were gone. I was alone, in the dark ward, unable to move my own body and with my hours-old healthy baby in a plastic crib beside me. I fell asleep.

I woke with a start. The baby was crying next to me. What on earth was I supposed to do? I still couldn't feel my legs and felt too weak to try to push myself up in order to scoop him up from the crib beside me. Apart from his weak wails, the ward was silent. I searched for a call button that I assumed must be there, to no avail. I could see it on the other side of the terrifically tall bedside cabinet, but I was metres away from being able to reach it. I gave up. The baby calmed down and I turned my head and went back into a profound sleep. My maternal instinct was not quite as voracious as the desperate need for my jaded body to recover, it seemed.

Next thing I knew, I was eating quite possibly the greatest white toast and hot butter I had ever eaten. I was ravenous. The ward was still quiet and the nurse helped me to get into a sitting position as I could still not feel my legs from the waist down. I was trying in vain to not let it worry me. I ate the toast and slurped the tea as if I had not eaten in months, rather than days. I kept peering to my left, to see the tightly wrapped-up bundle of white cloth that was cocooning my son. It was roughly 1,654 degrees in the ward. I was sweating with heat, shaking with adrenaline and crying with overwhelm, all while begging the kind nurse for more toast. The baby started to squeak and yet I still couldn't reach him. If I am honest, I wasn't trying too hard, as I had no idea at that point what was expected of me. Was I supposed to try to feed him again? Do you immediately change their nappy? Am I allowed to cuddle him in this tropical heat? Will I ever be able to sit up unaided again? Where is the toast?

The toast arrived and the nurse took the baby and cradled him while I snuffled into the life-saving carbs. She told me she would go and get a syringe to collect the colostrum that my nipples were producing. Colostrum is basically the cream at the top of gold-foil milk, the good stuff. However, all I heard was the word 'syringe'. My body was throbbing with pain and fatigue and yet there was talk of a fucking syringe. As ever, my face said what my mind was thinking and the nurse kindly explained it was a needleless syringe which would help collect the liquid. She showed me how to squeeze my nipple to try to extract the ivory nectar. I mean, I knew this would be hard and it is the most natural thing in the world, but are you fucking kidding me?

We had been squeezing away, with little regard to the pain, for what felt like at least fifteen minutes and had produced 2ml. Two millilitres. We tried to latch him on again, but he didn't even try to nestle in or root around, he simply forcibly pulled back and turned his head away. The second or third time I had ever held my darling boy and he was pulling away from me with much more strength than I had at that time. The palpable sense of disappointment and fear of not knowing what to do oozed out of me, and having read the room (by which I mean my bed within a room full of other beds, separated only by a curtain) the nurse offered to take care of the baby while I slept some more. Naps, do indeed, save lives.

A couple of hours later, having proved that I could wee and armed with a caseload of painkillers, my sister and I left the tropical heat of the hospital, swinging the heavy and bizarrely awkward to carry car seat with each step. I was leaving the building as a mother to a tiny, healthy Herbert. My son, born at 11.50 p.m. on my dad's birthday.

CHAPTER 6:
DONOR, NOT DAD

I want to start this chapter by saying that I really, truly don't want anything in the next few pages, or indeed in any part of this book, to sound anything like scaremongering. I just know that it would have really, truly helped me if I'd had my eyes opened to certain realities of motherhood – particularly the very early days of it – before I got there, rather than lapping up what Hollywood, books, social media and closed doors were feeding me in terms of how 'magical' it all is, with none of the fifty shades of shit brown in between. Sure, it can be absolutely magical if your idea of magic is from the Penn & Teller school of smoke and mirrors, but it is also – let's be honest – breathtakingly punishing.

I feel really strongly that prospective parents should have the ability to educate themselves on the full spectrum of everything that happens in those first few months after birth if they want to – from possible gut-wrenching tragedy to parental nirvana and the somewhere in between that most of us will find ourselves straddling, including the constant emotional push and pull all that can involve. I didn't delve far enough into all this before I had Herb, and while the outcome would inevitably have been the same even if I had, I also might have felt slightly less blindsided and a little more prepared. I had so desperately wanted a child, that I could only see everything about motherhood as being blissful, I had made myself totally blinkered to it's potential realities.

So, with that caveat, FUCK ME, I found it hard! So hard. So much harder than even the 'oh, you just wait' brigade could have warned me about. Granted, the 'oh, you just wait' crew would say it with a glint in their eye and something akin to a cartoon baddy's evil laugh, and I just wanted to prove those smug bastards wrong. Mainly I thought they were talking about lack of sleep being 'the issue', and that the rest of my day would be spent drowning in nauseous adoration for my charming offspring while devouring box set after box set. Turns out, all that babies mainly do for twenty-four hours a day, for a good few weeks, is a rotation of sleep, wake, cry, feed, wind, wee, poo and gurn, and yet they are absolutely ALL-CONSUMING.

It is extraordinary the pressure you feel when you are the sole person in charge of a miniature human, to ensure that both of you are thriving. This wasn't even the expectation of others, though, this was a bar that I had set far too high for myself in my inaugural and longed-for role of being someone's mum. Herb's mum. You see, he was no longer the baby with no face who was making me feel sick, whose kicks I would eagerly wait for, whose presence inside me made me feel whole. He was now my son, lying in my arms with my dried blood still on top of his head, my Herb. I owed it to him for us both to flourish. I had ached for these moments for years and yet, now they were here, I was drowning.

For the first six weeks, I was like a rabbit that had been catapulted into headlights, forever blinking furiously to try to regain my composure. I assumed, due to my mental health history, that I would be a prime candidate for some degree of postnatal depression, so I was acutely aware of every emotion coursing through my body. All 8,603 of them.

Stating that motherhood is beyond hard has become such a cliché, but even trying to move beyond the anecdotal eventually sounds trite. It

is a vicious circle of the indescribable because
it is so unique to each and every person, and
for each and every baby, and therefore to
characterise its full spectrum of emotional glory
without touching on clichés every now and again
is like trying not to tread on hot lava at the foot
of an active volcano. Just to be clear, I am very
probably going to tread on that lava. I make no
apologies for it, either, because the truth is, these
clichés are clichés for a reason. Motherhood
really will take you to the utter depths of your
emotions before launching you to euphoria all
within one simple fish-finger-strewn mealtime. So
me trying to keep my emotions in check and the
thought that I possibly had control of any of that
is vaguely comical.

My first day home from the hospital was magical
though, truly. I was so thrilled to be away from the
ward and out of the earshot of the other babies that
were making my boobs gorge in solidarity. Herb was
mainly sleeping and the house was perfectly calm.
My amazing sisters scuttled round me, making sure I
was comfortable, fed and watered. I now understand

why in many cultures there is a 'sitting in' period after childbirth where the mother and child are encouraged to stay in bed to heal, to learn to feed and grow accustomed to one another, while being nourished by family. This is in stark contrast to the UK, where we can sometimes be made to feel it is some sort of competition as to how quickly you can get back into jeans (I haven't owned any since the nineties) and how soon you took Little One for their first meal out. Motherhood isn't a competition. It is a wildly different experience for absolutely everyone.

Being at home with my sisters felt like my sitting-in period, my time for me and my boy. I was euphoric that I had done it. That I had made my dreams come true and I had walked back into my home, with all its relics of my past, cradling in my arms the hopes of my future. The future I had paved the way for on my own, like some sort of fucking incredible superhero. Honestly, in that moment I felt like I could rule the world. (If the world were a tired, 1930s semi in Oxford.) It soon became blooming obvious, though, that it was the pain relief that was making me feel that good, not necessarily the delirium of feeling that I had become the living embodiment of Girl Power. Like I was with the Spice Girls downing cocktails at Number Ten in 1996 while Tony Blair was riding the wave of Cool Britannia. Nope. It was in fact the well-known tipple of strong pain relief and raging hormones.

I couldn't stop staring at Herb, and while I knew I wanted him to be safe, warm, loved and nurtured, I can honestly say I didn't feel like I had been sucker-punched with maternal instinct and bottomless love. I had been so aware of my own sense of self prior to his long-awaited arrival, that the sudden dynamic change in feeling as if I was totally part of someone else, a newcomer to the world I had inhabited alone for so long, was really, really hard to acclimatise to. As the painkillers started to wear off, I was startled as to how much physical pain my body was in. Of course it was, it had just been through some quite serious trauma. It had been investigated, tugged, pulled, stroked, ripped, cut, pricked, stretched, drugged and stitched. In all the time I was pregnant, I had such tunnel vision about the pain of the labour that it had genuinely not once ever occurred to me that I would be in pain AFTER it, too. My naivety and, let's face it, evasion of the blinking obvious, was staggering to me as I look back, but I remember it being so shocking that when people described those early days as hard, it wasn't just about the baby's needs, it was about those of the person who had birthed that child.

My body ached and throbbed in a way I didn't know was possible. I felt like I had a hot baguette in between my thighs, my vagina had swollen and contorted so much. While I definitely wasn't going to rubberneck at the car crash down there, I can assure you it wasn't a case of out of sight and out of mind. When the midwife came for a home visit in the first week after leaving hospital, I honestly couldn't have got on my back on the sofa with my legs open quick enough, begging for her to tell me it was all OK down there. She assured me that I was healing beautifully. 'Beautifully' was the most comical description of what would have definitely looked apocalyptic. This poor young girl hadn't even been offered a cup of tea, just a full-frontal view of my wounded genitals!

I seriously couldn't believe it was normal to feel so intensely bewildered. Yet, I am here to tell you it absolutely is. While it is true that pendulum swings both ways, some people can feel vibrant and alive and energised at the wonder that has just happened to them, others, very much me included, feel like they are wading through treacle while their poor battered vagina trails behind!

THINGS I DIDN'T KNOW ABOUT TINY BABIES

- The smell of their warm head is the most wonderful scent in the world.
- They make thousands of hilarious involuntary limb movements every day that make them look like they are fighting the air.
- Winding is a ball ache that no one warns you about. It can take hours! (Tip: babies will often have a slight blue colouration above their top lip if they need winding. I learnt this from my amazing cousin who is a nurse at Great Ormond Street.)
- They are very rarely totally silent, they are nearly always snuffling and kerfuffling.
- When they first wrap their whole hand around your little finger you feel like you may burst with a love you never felt before.
- Babies have a really strong, strong grip and can pull your hair out in a flash, which I presume is why the 'Mum Bun' was invented.
- Cradle cap – looks absolutely gross, but is entirely normal . . . your baby isn't shedding their skin!

> • It is possible for them to arrive into this world looking like a hybrid between a wrinkly Winston Churchill and a skinned rabbit and miraculously transform into a tiny beautiful babbling human.

And yet, I'll admit that I feel like a bit of a fraud when I talk about these early days, as people assume I was all alone. In actual fact, I am 98 per cent sure I had it better than most people when they come home clueless with their first baby and their equally at a loss partner. I had two devoted sisters with the experience of bringing up six children between them who were sharing their (albeit sometimes a little rusty!) knowledge and assurance with me twenty-four hours a day. Literally. I often thought about how different it would have been if I had been in a relationship and we were both fumbling around blindfolded through those early days. I didn't ever have to compromise with exactly what I wanted in terms of who was in the house, no meddling mothers-in-law to appease. My sisters took turns to be with us, one driving the hour back to her young family and job and the other driving over two and a half hours each way to try to keep her deli open and running smoothly. I had no idea how good I had it. They would share night feeds with me and even allow me to sleep right through some nights when I needed it. I honestly believe those restorative hours of sleep are what allowed me to keep going through those initial few months.

I have no doubt that I wouldn't have been able to battle on had they not dug those feather-filled foundations for me. Yet still, from my gilded cage, I found those days impossible. I felt completely crushed by the weight of responsibility I had birthed and the looming inevitability that my sisters would soon return to their own lives.

I had wanted this life so very badly. I had ached and longed and reached and fought for this time, for me to be cradling my own tiny baby to sleep in the still, cold hours of the morning. I had yearned for this. For this very moment of sniffing the head of a baby that I had felt grow inside me, yet I was grappling round trying to find emotions other than pain and fear. I was letting us both down, I felt sure of it. The shock at the lack of instantaneous harmony within me felt brutal. I couldn't check the returns policy of the sperm bank. I couldn't hold my hands up to my friends, family, neighbours, doctors, Instagram and say, 'Hey guys, you know I have bored on for literally years about my primal urge to have a baby? Well, turns out I was an idiot. My primal urge is a complete twat. I want my money back. This is not for me. I am not going to be a good mother.'

I couldn't see a way out of it. I was very aware that my thoughts weren't dark and I never truly worried about the safety of Herb or me, but I felt so utterly lost and claustrophobic. I vividly remember realising that I would always have to be aware of the baby and where he was, what he was doing, if he was safe, even if I was just popping to the loo. In those evolving days, every tiny task seemed monumental. Yet I was surrounded by care and help. I shouldn't have felt this absent.

YOU ARE NOT ALONE

Since admitting how hard I found those first early days and weeks, I have had literally thousands of mums tell me they felt the same but were too scared of being judged to admit it. So please know that if you are feeling that way too, you are absolutely not the only mum to feel like they have made the wrong decision, that they won't

be a good mum, that they want their old life
back, that they are failing.

More importantly, you don't have to suffer in
silence, and you absolutely shouldn't do so,
either. If you are feeling desperate – seek help.
Talk to a doctor as soon as possible. They
will point you in the right direction to get the
support you need. You are not alone. You are
not a failure. You will not feel like this forever.
There is help, and it will get better.

I had assumed that because I had reached my pot of
gold at the end of the rainbow, I would perpetually be
floating on clouds, staring at my offspring like he was
the living embodiment of love and joy. I think other
people had assumed I would feel that way too, so no
one ever delved into how I was really doing, because
the 'Liv has finally had a baby' box had been ticked.
That is not to say that I didn't feel loved and cared for,
it is just that, like me, no one (except my sisters) was
really looking past the fact that I must be absolutely
bloody jubilant. I'd had clouds over much of my late
childhood and then my whole adult life and I genuinely thought they would part and the sun would shine

forever as soon as my baby was nestled in my arms. What an idiot!

The ridiculous thing was, Herb was such a good baby. He didn't have a huge, voracious cry, he was healthy, he seemed content, he was still bruised and looking like a 1930s bare-knuckle fighter but he slept and snuffled and moulded to his new environment with ease. I, however, felt like my body was never going to repair as I frantically sprayed lavender water up my vag every time I went to the loo, necked arnica tablets to speed up healing, ate more linseeds than seemed necessary to help with The Poo and checked the list of pain-relief timings every three minutes to see if I could legitimately take any more yet. I also had to take heparin injections every day because I was at high risk of clotting and I couldn't fathom that my body had to go through any more affliction. I was, as ever, being a spoilt brat, just like I had been as a teenager. I wanted my cake and to eat it painlessly too.

The spring sun shone through the window and my baby lay sleeping soundly by my side in a pristine white babygrow, my sisters busying themselves with making endless drinks that I was able to consume while they were still hot, offering up rounds of bacon sarnies, ploughing through mountains of washing and reading up on when we should bath him for the first time. If you had peered through the window, the scene would have looked blissful. And yet, while the house was relatively calm, my body and mind felt like an absolute whirlwind of emotions and anguish. The days were long, albeit filled with very little to do other than learning about being a mother, staring at lists of feed times, typing frantic 2 a.m. WhatsApp messages to my NCT group with panicked questions about room temperatures and generally trying to acclimatise to my new role.

Three weeks after Herb was born, I turned thirty-nine. I decided that would be a great day to register his birth and to take all three of my birthing team out to lunch to say thank you for going above and beyond. I was so excited to be going out with my full team. I washed my hair, put on a new dress, made myself smell of something other than hot milk, and with my sisters I jubilantly went to the registry office to tell the world that I had become a mother. Walking into the stale air of these council rooms was a huge anti-climax. I mean, I had been there before, so I am not sure what I was expecting, but it definitely felt like a pretty lacklustre way to announce to the world the arrival of a child.

A smiley lady came through the door and called my name. My sisters remained in the waiting room and

I completed a very clumsy twenty-four-point turn of my vast pushchair housing my tiny child and tried to catch up with the lady who strode through the greying corridors at a pace, swiping open key-fob-locked doors with ease as she went.

I sat down and we went through some pleasantries. She congratulated me and recorded the details of his birth, followed by his name: Herbert Leonard Elvis. Wow, she remarked, let's hope he's a character. I was both taken aback and thrilled in equal measure. Yes of course, and I wanted him to be a character, and thank god I had clearly given him a name that wasn't so middle-of-the-road that it warranted such exclamation. I was asked if I was his mother. Yes, yes. My details were then offered up. Then suddenly she said, 'And Herbert's father, is he here today?' OH MY GOD. My mind blew up into a frenzy. What if he wasn't allowed to exist if he didn't have a dad? What if we would have to go to court to prove his existence? What if I had to move to Denmark? OH MY FUCKING GOD. I stumbled over my words and explained that he didn't actually have a dad, he had a donor. I waited for the complication. However, she just continued to type without so much as a missed beat.

The hairs stood up on my arms and I put my little finger into Herb's hand by way of reassurance that he was in fact real. What seemed like minutes of missed heartbeats later, she declared that her friend had had a donor baby and what a great decision I had made. I cried. In that moment, my hormones were coursing through me and a civil servant had just seemed to validate my decision. And then the emotions just took hold. I wept as I picked Herb up from his pram in that grand yet unkempt office to give him a congratulatory hug. We had made it! Our family was legit. I got myself together and placed him back in his bassinet, then awkwardly manoeuvred the ridiculous pram back the way I came and regrouped with my sisters.

We walked out of those filthy offices into the hot May sunshine and took photos to commemorate my son being an official member of society. With a spring in my step, we went to have a celebratory birthday and birth-registering day lunch in my favourite restaurant. This turned out to be a complete disaster, of course! The restaurant is a conservatory, it was about 34 degrees and my son evidently did not in any way like being hot. Such is motherhood – highs and lows in a matter of hours. But my god, what a birthday; how wonderful it was to be able to spend it with my boy as an official team.

A month in, and the endless generous gifts that had been sent by family and friends started to slow down, the initial kerfuffle of my sister and me trying to bath Herb in an odd sort of half-upright barrel contraption became a smooth process with something less modern, his poo was no longer the swamp green of the first few days and the rhythm of daily life began to settle . . . and then suddenly they were gone. My sisters had the audacity to go back to their daily lives and families, leaving me to look after my own child single-handed!

TIPS FOR PREPARING FOR LIFE WITH A NEWBORN AS A SOLO MUM

- Practise with your buggy. Seriously. Nothing can get you more flustered than endless levers and buckles when a newborn is screaming in your ear and you need fresh air. Same goes with a sling. Practise. Practise. Practise.

- Draw up a list of people who will happily take your call at 3.17 a.m. when you are in an inexplicable but very real panic about the temperature of the bedroom. Make a rota if you have to.

- Have a basket in each room that you will be using with everything you will need in it, so you don't have to move if the baby is asleep on you.
- Fill your freezer (don't forget the veg). Stock your wine fridge!
- Book supermarket delivery slots as far in advance as you can. You will thank yourself when everything else takes over.
- Don't binge-watch everything on Netflix/Audible, you are just about to spend quite a lot of time at home alone, so you need to make sure you have some cracking shows/books waiting for you.
- Declutter your house if you can (I am a hoarder so I had a lot I could get rid of) as your house is just about to be filled with baby 'stuff'. . . even if you don't want it to!
- Read all the parenting books that interest you or that you have been recommended as they will feel daunting in their vastness once the baby has arrived.
- Get your hair cut. It may be a couple of months before you are able to go again.
- Buy some really good bed linen, you are going to spend a lot of time there, so you want to make it feel like a little luxury.

- If you have space and the finances, invest in a tumble dryer. I still envy anyone with a tumble dryer.
- Practise and perfect a few simple recipes you can make with your eyes closed within fifteen minutes, preferably from store cupboard ingredients – and make sure the cupboard is full. A perfect one is Caramelized Shallot Pasta by Alison Roman. It is a game changer!

Jesus Christ, was I ready for this? Was he ready for this? Having my team around me had been like a constant safety net. If Herb wouldn't settle in the depths of the night, one of their faces would appear round my bedroom door to check I wasn't in a panic. If I was hungry there was always food in the fridge, the milk was in date, the endless babygrows were laundered, the visitors were heavily screened, the Marmite toast was in constant supply, assurances were given and hands were held. The love they both had for this tiny little boy who they had known for only a few short weeks was palpable. Then they were gone.

The first night I spent alone with Herb, he was only around ten days old, and I felt pride and fear in equal measure. I knew that I had to be doing OK if my sisters had deemed it a good idea to leave me alone with my son, and yet what would happen if I needed them, if he didn't stop crying or his poo turned blue or I wanted a shower? But I knew this was it, the moment I'd been working towards of being a family, the two of us. Now I just had to make sure that we were OK, Herb and I, together. There was nothing spiritual or enlightening about what happened next, no mood boards or manifesting. I just put my big, big girls' pants on and got stuck in. I was terrified.

Herb was asleep when they left and I settled down to enjoy our time alone. I had spent so much of my adult life alone at home, with Elvis, that adapting to having people around me for numerous weeks had felt nearly as bizarre as the fact that I had a son. I was heavy with tiredness; my body may not have hurt so much anymore but my mind was still coming to terms with this new life. We made it through our first night alone together triumphantly, and we have been doing so ever since.

I had heard numerous times the sage advice that I should sleep when the baby sleeps. Who were these people doling out such 'wisdom'? How was that even possible? It might, potentially, be feasible if you had a Dermot or a Daisy (or two adoring sisters!) downstairs doing the washing, the cooking, the life admin, the bottle cleaning, the organising, the dog walking, the just-sitting, the putting the bins out, the fridge filling, the showering, the bill paying, the batch cooking, the endless scrolling of Google to second-guess your every maternal move. If you were on your own, though, those were the snippets of time you had to get your shit together, because what I learnt is that to feel well in my mind, I had to feel on top of everything that I actually did have control over – i.e. not Herb.

So I set about trying to make my life as seamless as possible. This involved various levels of mundane organisation that I had never thought I would be capable of, pre-baby. One of my most useful tips to any new mother is that I placed baskets around the house that housed a plethora of useful shit I might need at any given moment – nappies, wipes, muslins, nappy cream, nipple cream, crisps (always, always crisps), bottles of water, dog treats, lip balm, phone charger, a magazine, a pen, a small blanket, some thank-you cards (still unwritten), painkillers, vests, clean babygrows and some toys. There were three of these baskets – one in the living room, one in the kitchen and one in my bedroom. I became obsessed with them. I was convinced they were going to keep everything in order and make everything easier. You know what? They did. Having them always within arm's reach meant that there was no scurrying around frantically trying to find a muslin to wipe up the sick dripping down my back while Herb screamed. It meant I could have something to eat and drink if he fell asleep on me. It meant I just knew where everything we needed was. I still use those baskets, they just have more dinosaurs in now.

I also made sure that I bought enough babygrows that I didn't need to do washing every day. No one, absolutely no one, wants to be doing washing and finding radiator space for drying your pants when you are so tired you genuinely have to pause to remember the name of your newborn. Amazing friends had bought me COOK vouchers, which were an absolute godsend, along with my magic freezer that was full to bursting with meals that I had batch-cooked pre-Herb. This meant that as soon as the baby was down 'for the night', I didn't have to think about what I would cook, I could just shove some great meals in the oven to heat up, whack out an Almond Magnum and some fruit and watch half an hour of TV before going to bed at 8 p.m., to get a head start on the night ahead. It was wild. Yet I never felt alone. I felt lost, bewildered, strong, tired, lonely, proud, anguished, but never alone. I had started to feel as though Herb and I were a team, totally in it together. One of us was clearly pulling much more weight than the other, but nonetheless, it was the dawn of our small but mighty team.

GREAT PRESENTS TO BUY FRIENDS WHO HAVE HAD A BABY ALONE

My best advice is to ask them what they need, rather than assume you know what they want.

- Vouchers for your time to babysit – allowing them some time alone is the best gift. Likewise, time away from the baby with you. So perhaps one friend can babysit while the other takes you out for dinner/a coffee. It is a win for everyone, including the friend doing the babysitting as they are getting time away from their own family!
- Meal vouchers/home-cooked meals – a full freezer is an absolute game-changer.
- A doula – sounds ridiculous, but I have heard of large groups of friends clubbing together for postnatal doula time. This would be gold dust to any new mother.

- Your support – a real, true and genuine offer to answer their phone call in the middle of the night if they are worried, desperate or alone.
- Buy anything that will make THEM feel good – chocolate, a candle, Spacemasks, a massage voucher (with babysitting), a haircut, a bottle of their favourite tipple. Let other people buy the baby clothes that will never get worn!
- A coffee machine with pod subscription.
- A list of your favourite TV series/podcasts that they may not have watched but could catch up on.
- Not for when the baby is born, but remember your single-parent friends on Mother's/Father's Day, Valentine's, Christmas and their birthday and think of something you can get them 'from' their babe – even just a card. It will mean the world.

The other key member of our team was Elvis, and I needed to know he was being looked after just as much as Herb was. So when I was pregnant I spoke to an amazing dog behaviourist, Louise from The Darling Dog Company, so that I could make sure I didn't do anything 'wrong' in terms of bringing a baby into Elvis's life. Elv had had my full attention for nearly a decade, was rarely left alone and he knew he was the centre of my world. I didn't want to unwittingly do anything that would make him feel uncomfortable or, worse, as my sisters pointed out, jealous. He is the most placid dog in the world, some days it is all I can do to get him to go for a walk, and he runs away from cats in sheer terror, so I wasn't wildly worried about his behaviour towards a baby, but I didn't want to take any chances.

Anyway, I spent an hour on the phone to Louise, talking about Elvis and the bomb I was just about to chuck into his world, and she shared some absolute gems of wisdom that I wouldn't even have thought about. Two of these were absolute gamechangers. One was for Elvis not to be home when I brought the baby back from the hospital, which was the absolute opposite of what I would have done! Having listened to our usual routine, her view was that the moment I came back from the hospital Elvis would have been excited and I would have been tired and protective of the baby – I might have snapped at Elvis in that moment, or sent him to his bed, automatically starting our little family off on the wrong foot. So instead, my friend Mark had Elv for a few days when I was in labour and when he brought him back a day or two later, I was showered, rested and calm. As it happened, Elv didn't even notice Herb was there for a good hour, so there was no frantic meeting, just a calm, steady sniff and a little lick of his feet! Obviously this is what worked for us having consulted Louise about our circumstances, it could be different for everyone.

The other thing that would never have dawned on me was to arrange for people to walk Elvis for the first month. That way, if I fancied a walk, I could take him and it would be a bonus, but if my mind or body couldn't face it then it didn't matter as someone else could. Genius! I lived next to a beautiful meadow that was accessed via my street, so finding people to pick him up was never a problem. One of my neighbours' daughters was completing her Duke of Edinburgh Award and she had to win her 'Helpful Elf' badge or something similar, so she offered to walk Elvis for me a good three or four times a week for a few months. It was incredible. The days I needed someone else to walk him I would literally just wait for someone to pass by the house, open the front door and ask if they would take Elv with them. On a couple of occasions, I even gave them Herb! They thought they were going to have a nice quiet walk on the meadow with their dogs and they would end up with mine and a fresh baby! I wouldn't ask strangers, of course, I knew nearly everyone in the village or, at the very least, I knew the name of their dog, so sending Herb off with them for an hour while I snuck upstairs for a nap was the greatest luxury I could have asked for. I am so bloody grateful to everyone in that village for their generous support through those times, they really were all lifesavers.

It was about that time that it dawned on me that I really did have to ask for help when I needed it. When people offer their time, you often just bat it off with platitudes, but I absolutely had to learn that they meant it. I also had to learn to take them up on it. I have never been very good at asking for help, opting instead for the truly brilliant 'bury your head in the sand' approach to nearly everything. Yet now it wasn't about me. If there were any ramifications, they weren't mine alone anymore. I was sharing my load with Herb. So if I became too tired to function, or my mental health deteriorated, he would also be suffering. It was imperative I stopped being so bloody British and instead asked for help/accepted help/sought help whenever I needed it. This is still a steep learning curve for me, even three years down the line, but back then I was so desperate for composure that I didn't bat an eyelid when I screamed from my driveway 'PLEASE CAN YOU TAKE HERB AND ELV WITH YOU!' to families going on walks. I knew they understood; they knew how hard it was, they had seen inside that particular Pandora's Box, and 98.7 per cent of the time they were all too thrilled to be able to pay it forward.

First up in my lesson on asking for help was contacting my lovely cousin, who in all honesty I am not particularly close to and who I would see once every five years or so. She is a paediatric nurse at Great Ormond Street Hospital and such a kind and genuine person that I knew if I reached out, she would want to help. She seemed thrilled I had called and she came to stay. Having her calm and giggling presence for those few days when I really needed them was wonderful. I was quickly learning that the benefits of asking for help far outweighed the awkwardness of admitting you needed it. I knew that this need for additional hands wasn't going to solely be for when Herb was tiny, but we would need the love, guidance and support of a loyal band of buddies for the rest of our days! So, in came The Godparents. I am lucky enough to have four godparents, a couple of whom I am really close to to this day. One in particular, my wonderful Auntie Ann, has been a pillar of support, guidance and general hilarity to me since Mum died. I felt really strongly that I wanted Herb to have this sort of relationship with my friends too. Not in case the worst should happen to me, but because our immediate family of just two could do with being expanded by a couple of people, if not by blood, then by a loving tie to bind them. Never knowingly not doing anything by halves, I decided Herb should have nine such people. Yep, nine. Why go small when you can go big? I decided he should have the same amount of godparents as me, plus one for each grandparent and parent he was without. I wanted his team to have an abundance of skills they could teach him that I can't. I wanted him to feel at home at their houses. I wanted him to know that he can call them in the middle of the night when he is in trouble at university. I wanted him to know they will whisk him away for a pub lunch to whinge about how embarrassing I am as a mum. I wanted him to know he would be invited on their annual family panto trip (God knows, I am not going to take him! Oh no I'm not!) and not feel like the odd one out. I wanted him to know they were his family. Thankfully I am #blessed with the best friends in the land. All for their own special reasons.

Of course, there was always going to be a huge, sparkly blue-eyed hole where my Jen should have been, but it has been filled in (not replaced) by her wonderful brother Harry. Herb doesn't know it yet, but he is the luckiest kid in town. All I have to do is learn to lean on his team when I know both Herb and I need it the most.

THINGS TO PUT THE GODPARENTS/GUARDIANS/FAIRIES IN CHARGE OF:

Herb has MANY godparents. I have asked them to all be in charge of teaching Herb various life skills, such as:

- Dancing like no one is watching.
- How to host a great party.
- How to create a playlist of dreams.
- Sartorial elegance.
- The finer points of the rules of rugby/football/tennis/cricket.
- DIY (I literally cannot be trusted).
- The importance of afternoon naps.
- To be the last man standing at parties.
- To love unconditionally.
- To surprise people with cards to remind them that you love them.
- To encourage passions wholeheartedly.
- To never, ever, ever accept second best.
- How to cook a stash of favourite, go-to recipes.

The other person who has an innate ability to know when I need help and who lives close enough to offer it to me is my sister Annie. So when she asked if I wanted her to look after Herb, overnight, at her house, I bit her arm off! I think Herb was about three weeks old and I know that to some people they could not imagine being away from their young baby, but I felt like I was in urgent need of space. Of air. Just one night to regroup and breathe – without Herb. My sister could not believe that I had agreed and kept asking if I was sure. Absofuckinglutely I was! The way I saw it was that she was not a stranger, she was a mother herself and had done all of this before (even if this was a bit of a refresher course!), Herb had spent 80 per cent of his life in her company so far, she held him before I did, she idolised him – and I idolised sleep.

We met in an Asda car park midway between our houses to do the handover. It must have looked hilarious to anyone who saw me hand over this tiny baby and all his worldly belongings to someone who then drove off into the distance with him. I felt so strange when I saw her taillights disappearing off, out of sight, and I couldn't work out if it was anxiety or euphoria.

All I knew was that that twenty-minute trip around Asda felt like a bloody spa holiday. I nipped in and out with just my keys and a purse – there was no massive pram, no kerfuffle, no straps, no huge rucksack of stuff 'just in case'. Just me, my battered body, my keys, my purse, 200 strangers and aisles and aisles of stuff I didn't need but that I could peruse over with no thought for anyone else. It. Was. Glorious. Who knew Asda was such nirvana?

On the way home I stopped off at the chippie (again, just nipping in felt so bizarre) to drown my body in carbs. Then, once home, I cleared up, put a wash on and went to bed. I think it was about 2 p.m. All I know is, when I woke up, over sixteen hours later, I felt unbelievable. Like I'd had an absolute lease of life, like I could take on the world. It was that day, having been apart from Herb for less than twenty-four hours, when he was back in my arms, that I knew I loved him. I really, deeply loved him.

It was such a relief. I had been so worried that that feeling would never come. That actually I wasn't the maternal person I thought I was. That this had all been a really grave mistake. That it would probably be best for Herb if I wasn't his mum. Then suddenly, after just a few hours apart, it dawned on me while I was scrolling through the 37,789 photos of him that I'd taken in just the very few weeks of his life so far, that I was aching to see him, that I would do anything to protect that little boy, that he was the sum of all my parts and I was totally bloody in love with him.

Falling in love with my son is not to suggest that life was suddenly effortless. It was probably the opposite, actually. Every time, every single time that I thought I had my shit together, another curve ball would trip me up. These curve balls, I quickly learnt, were called developmental leaps. Holy sweet Jesus, it felt like driving blindfolded. You know how to drive, you knew where the pedals were, yet why the fuck were the roads suddenly upside down?

There are about eight developmental leaps in a baby's first year and they happen when the babe is learning something new, like when they start to realise that it is THEIR hand that they are looking at or when they learn about the relationship between objects, so you moving further away from them may cause them distress that they wouldn't have noticed before. I am sure these leaps are terribly important to the emotional growth of my child and everything, but honestly, they were so tough. Thankfully I had been told about an app called The Wonder Weeks, that tracks your baby's leaps, so you can tell when they are coming. The app would generate a graph and the leaps would be illustrated by whacking great big thunderbolts. You could see into the future, too, so that you had a bit of an inkling as to when the thunderbolts were lurking round the corner. So your cute, giggling, cuddly bundle of joy would suddenly turn into a wriggly, whingey, irritable ball of rage. The great thing was the app would assure you, you weren't doing anything 'wrong', that you hadn't accidentally picked up someone else's child when you nipped out for nappies. It was still your child, it was just your child being deeply unreasonable and angry at the world! Yeah, sure, they were learning and growing and developing all their emotional and physical behaviours, but they were also being truly irrational while they did it!

What was worse was that some of these leaps could last for weeks – they felt like years, but apparently they were only weeks. I just had to buckle up and cross off the days on a calendar that offered no chocolate or sweets behind doors as a reward. I honestly think that if I hadn't have known about these leaps, I would have thought I was losing my mind, because the difference in Herb at every single one was vast.

So why then did I think it was a good idea to go to a festival with him when he was about six weeks old? Do you know why? Because I hadn't realised The Power of the Leap by that stage. Look, I wasn't going to Glastonbury for a week or anything, I was going to a two-day festival in Oxford with no camping, VIP access and nearly my entire family with me. At that stage I was basically living like Beyoncé, taking my full entourage with me whenever I left the house. No Jay-Z in sight. Herb and I were just getting into the swing of life together and then I go and throw something stupid like a festival into the works.

The thing I learnt pretty quickly about my boy is, very much like his mother, he absolutely hates being hot. So there we were, in the middle of an open field, in what was the hottest summer since 1453 or something. I hadn't ever really been anywhere crowded with him before, but I was determined to prove I could do it (with my family of Sherpas in attendance, of course!) and we were going to have a really cracking day out, too. I don't know who I thought I needed to prove myself to. My sister and my nieces were just thrilled to be able to see him and to have a day out, and I can't imagine anyone else in that field even remotely gave a toss about the fact that I had a baby with me. Herb was jiggling around in his pram as I looked around for somewhere to sit, when I realised I should probably have brought him some ear defenders. The place was littered with nice families, with their nice children playing excitedly, wearing nice ear defenders. Whereas my tiny six-week-old bean was turning purple in the heat and would have to cope with the aural onslaught of Elvana (you didn't know you needed an Elvis-fronted Nirvana tribute act in your life, did you?). So I had basically failed at the first hurdle, hadn't I? I was shit at motherhood.

My sister doesn't tolerate defeatist attitudes like mine, so she swiftly took control and she found us some shade, we drank cold beers, we ate delicious food-truck delicacies and watched the world go by. The sound system was far enough away to alleviate any fear I had about Herb's wee ears and he lay on a rug, surrounded by his favourite people, with passers-by cooing over his cute tiny body wriggling around under the shady tree branches. When we got home, I felt really giddy at having been out with my son, and immediately planned to go again with him the next day, on our own, via a swift Amazon Prime ear-defenders haul. The following morning, I packed up all our belongings – literally all of them – and drove to as near to the site of the festival as possible. I pushed him through the field, passing another couple of families with tiny babies. Yep, I didn't need help. I could do this alone. Wait? What? What did those babies have on their ears? Cool. Cool. The reason Herb absolutely HATED having his hurriedly purchased ear defenders on was because I had bought ones for a three-year-old. They took up his whole head. The guilt was unbelievable. I couldn't bring myself to take him into the site again without protecting his literally tiny ears, so I found a tree just outside the hoardings and set us up underneath the dappled sunshine coming through her huge branches, the music audible but distant. Paul Simon came on (the reason I had bothered to remove myself from our homely bubble), and my baby and I danced together all the way through the *Graceland* album. I cried. I was so happy. I had done it. I had only gone and bloody done it. Herb, however, was livid in the sticky heat. But swings and roundabouts, at least one of us was happy as a clam.

MOST RIDICULOUS MIDDLE-OF-THE-NIGHT AMAZON PURCHASES BY A NEW MUM*

*me
- A fart reliever – for the baby, not me.
- A contraption that meant he wouldn't be able to roll over in bed.
- A 'tummy time' pillow – it is the same as any other pillow, just more expensive.
- 8 thermometers – you can never be too sure.

- Rescue Remedy (for me, not Herb!) – this won't touch the sides.
- A snot sucker – you won't believe you are typing the words, then suddenly sucking snot from a tiny baby seems totally normal.
- A breast pump – I wasn't breastfeeding.
- At least twelve books on 'baby routines' – I didn't have the energy to read one.

I had truly believed I would be a really relaxed 'let's just see how the day pans out/ what the baby wants' sort of mother. Again, actually becoming a mother showed me how very, very wrong I had been in my rose-tinted, pre-vagina-ripping days. Fairly early on before they left me to fend for myself, my sisters suggested perhaps I should look into following some sort of routine. I guffawed. Why would I need a routine? I am such a super-chill person that I can easily go with the flow and take what the babe throws at me.

Who the fuck was I kidding?

Well, certainly not my sisters. We bought a few books that they had remembered from their days of early motherhood and they (note: not me!) re-read them to get a gist of some little gems of information that would help us get through the day. Let me tell you, some of them were truly bonkers. Absolutely terrifying, almost dictating times throughout the day when you could nip for a wee. While I was desperately searching for The Answer to motherhood, to make this all seem as breezy as some people purported to find it (NB: there is no answer), I knew that I wasn't a scheduled-wee kind of girl. I was still not convinced I was a routine sort of parent, either. My darling Jen, before she died, would often say things like, 'Oh I will be round at 11.47 as the baby will be awake then for sixty-four minutes before he is due a feed and I need to put him down again, so we will have to leave by 1.17.' I would roll my eyes and laugh at her, telling her to just come and go as she pleased, I was easy breezy. Turns out that, now I was in her brilliant shoes, I most certainly wasn't easy or breezy.

It was beginning to dawn on me that perhaps, maybe, just possibly, I might like some sort of structure in my life, even if that meant I knew that I was doing it 'right' (NB: again, there is no right, ignore absolutely anyone who tells you there is).

So I made yet more 2 a.m. Amazon purchases for various books, and my ever-capable and devoted sisters and I sifted out some more little gems that we thought sounded like a good plan and blindly tried to apply them all to my life at the same time. Needless to say, some things worked, some things were a disaster, but, crucially, I never panicked. My sisters would just quickly comfort me and busy themselves with finding something else we could perhaps try.

When one of my godsons (now a strapping teenager) was born, his parents had a doula. At that time I had never, ever heard of such a thing. It turns out they are miracle workers and a knowledgeable reassuring presence you need in your life when you are fumbling around with a tiny human. They are a little like a hybrid of a non-medically trained handholder, comforter, imparter of knowledge, coupled with a reassuring best friend. Anyway, when I met my godson's doula all those years ago, I was absolutely fascinated by everything she created with her hands and every word that fell from her mouth. It just seemed like such a huge privilege to have someone so nurturing with you when you were at your most vulnerable. Back then I absolutely *knew* I would have a doula when I had my longed-for huge brood. I mean, obviously I didn't realise that fifteen years later I may not be able to afford such a teacher in my life, let alone not have a partner. Anyway, I had my sisters, who were inexplicably doing this for free! There was one thing I had always hung on to that the amazing doula had taught my friend – that night-time was bedtime for the baby.

It seems like a painfully obvious realisation, but I absolutely bloody loved the fact that I knew something I wanted to impart to my baby. So pretty much from week one, at 7 p.m., I would feed, change and swaddle Herb and place him in his little sleep pod and put him somewhere dark and quiet. This was always near me, obviously, but nonetheless I made sure that the vibe of the house changed to something like calm come 7 p.m. He seemed to love it, too, and would settle quickly, even if it wasn't to sleep, he would just be content to be flicking his little eyes around, taking everything in. Not long after, a friend with four children told me of a book she had always used to establish the basis of some form of routine that she had found really useful. When I bought it, I realised it was written by my godson's doula. What are the chances? So I lapped up every word, and in order to try to make my life as serene as possible during those halcyon days, I started in earnest to wrap a routine around our little family.

BOOKS I HAVE LOVED ABOUT PARENTING (N.B. MAINLY I HAVE LISTENED TO THE AUDIO BOOKS OF THESE)

- The Sensational Baby Sleep Plan, Alison Scott-Wright (AKA The Doula of Dreams!)
- Parenting the Sh*t out of Life, Mother Pukka, Papa Pukka
- What Have I Done?, Laura Dockrill
- Your Baby Week by Week, Simone Cave, Dr Caroline Fertleman
- The Book You Wish Your Parents Had Read, Philippa Perry
- My Wild and Sleepless Nights, Clover Stroud
- The Great Big Book of Families, Mary Hoffman, Ros Asquith

It turns out, I bloody love routine! The house felt calm and restorative. Everyone who has ever known me will laugh at the fact that I thought I wouldn't like the familiarity that it would bring me, as I am so very clearly someone who needs structure, that it is nothing short of comical that I thought for even a hot second I could fly by the seat of my pants. Herb and I thrived on our little routine. I knew my Jen would be looking down on me gently laughing, 'I told you so, my Livvy, I told you so.' Motherhood really does strip you naked and make you take a cold, hard, magnifying look at yourself, whether you want it to or not. It makes you get up close, too close, to all your flaws and demons, and demands you look them square in the eye, no matter how uncomfortable it makes you feel.

As with literally every single tiny part of parenthood, having a routine is not something that will work for everyone, or feel fitting for all broods. It may even be that it worked for one of your kids, but not another. However, for Herb, Elv and me, it was a game changer. A real bloody lifeline. Look, I didn't follow that book religiously and I certainly didn't follow it verbatim, but I did take from it what I needed in order to feel like I was flourishing. It felt like someone had handed me a black-and-white map; a map with hundreds of routes, hundreds of modes of transport, hundreds of destinations and hundreds of timetables, and all I needed to do was colour it in to suit my taste and pick any of the available journeys that would leave me feeling calm, at ease and, most imperative of all for me, very much like I had the upper hand over my life.

Once I had found a plan of attack that seemed to be working for Herb and me, it meant that even when the bastard developmental leaps popped up, I felt equipped to mentally handle them. Don't get me wrong, I still cried and swore and carbed up, but I didn't panic, I didn't freefall and I didn't give up. It also meant that I could reap the benefits of the new and unfamiliar pillars of my fledgling lifestyle: delegation and structure.

Our continued daily routine was working well for us, and knowing when Herb was likely to need a feed and be savvy to the fact that he seemed to be a fairly content tot, allowed me to come up with a genius delegation plan that would give me the greatest gift of all. Sleep. Essentially, I would feed Herb and put him to bed, I would then gorge on a freezer meal and go to bed soon after. Then at around ten or eleven o'clock, knowing that he was due another feed imminently, my friends and neighbours would be asked to let themselves in, bring Herb downstairs, feed him, burp him, change his nappy, bring him back upstairs, let Elv out for a wee and then let themselves out. That way I could very easily get a solid block of around six or seven hours of golden, therapeutic and uninterrupted sleep before the next middle-of-the-night feed. What a fucking gift! A life-saving, mind-altering, game-changing gift that my friends were giving me. Much like a lot of couples do, yet I wasn't part of a couple, I was a small part of a massive team. One of his godmothers would even come much earlier than his feed was due, just so she could spend longer with him! New motherhood cliché #641: it takes a village.

I know that at the time when it all felt so hard, I was so often told to 'treasure these moments', as those early days would so quickly pass. I really wanted to punch people who said that to me. A quick left hook and a swift kick in the shins. Really? I would really treasure feeling like a shell of my former self while trying to raise a child to be a great human, alone, not remembering where I last left my limbs or knowing if I could survive solely on vitamin supplements and Marmite? Sure. Course I would. I would repeatedly ask friends how old their children were so I could mentally count down the days until it looked like it may become gratifying. However, cliché #895 is wholly bloody true; I would unquestionably love to go back to that time now, with my eyes wide open, and to sniff that funny little wriggling baby once more.

I think it is imperative at this point to wholeheartedly assure new parents, single or otherwise, who have not had the benefit of hindsight gifted to them yet, that they too WILL survive. They will come out the other side of the dense fog without even realising it one day, and suddenly everything will have slotted into place – not neatly, it will all be in a huge heap – but it will be your heap and you will cherish it, even more if you created that glorious heap all by yourself.

CHAPTER 7:
THE JUGGLE
STRUGGLE

With every passing day, even the ones that seemingly never ended, it felt like I had finally been able to place myself within my new reality. My confidence as a mum and ultimately as an adult grew exponentially from those fresh foggy days that felt like a maze of nappies, laundry and various bodily fluids (not all Herb's!). I learnt to wear a life jacket of thick skin at all times, so that I was prepared for the next side swipe that parenting was going to bestow on me – and those side swipes came thick and fast. They still do.

There is always, always, something new to grapple with, to scrutinise, to accomplish, to fine-tune. Just as I was really beginning to relish this time with Herb, when I would clench my jaw so tight with passion as I squeezed his little thighs that I thought I would break my teeth, I had to think about going back to work. Obviously, I was the only one who was bringing in a wage to our little household and while I had saved (by which I mean had the advantage of being able to remortgage my home) some money for maternity, there was still a gaping hole in my funds that had been left by the shenanigans with the cowboy builder. I had tried to take him to court but he didn't answer the summons, meaning to take it further I would have had to pay a lot of money I didn't have in legal fees. I couldn't risk losing more.

Ultimately, while my naive fantasy was to stay home on maternity leave for one year, it was clear that just wasn't in any way possible financially, even with a hugely generous gift from my brilliant brother – especially when I started to look into the true cost of childcare. What a huge, cold, wet fish around the face of a reality check that was!

This felt like one of those times I could have really benefited from the encouragement of a partner. Maybe encouragement isn't even the right word, I just needed someone to advise me, to talk it all through with me, to help me make the right decision about who was going to look after my baby, and where and when. Logistically, it all seemed like absolute madness. I started by asking my friends about their experiences and what they would recommend. Guess what? Cliché #963 of parenting: there is no right answer; all children, all circumstances, are different. A little like the fantasy I have about meeting my husband, which involves a stranger knocking at my door, 'Hi, I am Dave, I am your husband,' and us living happily ever after in a field with some Bernese mountain dogs. I don't want any of the preamble, I don't want any of the 'oh, I wonder if he likes me and will text me back' bollocks, I just want it sorted.

Childcare felt like that for me. Yet, unlike finding a husband, there was no way I could just back away and ignore it. I simply had to go to work. Herb had to have childcare. It is not like my doting darling mum was going to swoop down from the Pearly Gates and scoop Herb up to bake cakes with him while I tried to earn us a great standard of living. My friends, family and neighbours had all been amazingly supportive so far, popping in and helping in shifts and sharing the load, but this was too big a load to ask any of them to take on permanently. There was no alternative: paying cold hard cash in exchange for caring for my baby five days a week was my only option.

Stupidly, I hadn't extensively looked into the cost of childcare before I had Herb, I just knew it was 'quite expensive' because I had heard people discussing it. It is just they were discussions I ignored because they had nothing to do with me. I shouldn't have ignored them, I should have taken bloody notes. When I was in my twenties, my sister lived in France, and I remember that in the particular town she lived in you only paid one euro per child per hour for childcare, as the local mayor topped up the fund or something. I know that back in the UK at that time there were gasps of wonder as she related this information, at how reasonable this French way of living was, and how wonderful it was that they helped mothers go back to work. I remember thinking that even if I lived there, I was sure I wouldn't need this great cheap childcare scheme, as I would likely be staying at home looking after my brood while Dave worked to keep a beautiful roof over our heads.

What a twat! It had never once occurred to me that I may have to do it alone, that someone else caring for my children while I worked might be my only option.

The dated parental narrative of work and gender roles is so ingrained that I can say, hand on heart, that for years I hadn't even contemplated an alternative. Naivety of this scale is why I am

so passionate about amplifying the realities
of parenthood like mine – like single fathers,
like adoption, like neuro-diversity, like blended
families, like multi-racial families, like surrogate
families, like LGBTQ+ families, like non-binary
families. This list of 'alternatives' is, and should
rightly be, an endless one. It truly isn't a
2.4-children, white-picket-fence world anymore.
That is not to say that that world shouldn't
exist – it absolutely should – but it should
co-exist with ease alongside the rainbow of
other family set-ups that people are living in,
too. Stories need to be told, to be listened to,
to be understood, so that when people like me
decide to walk past the picket fence, they do it
with pride and confidence in their own lifestyle,
with their eyes wide open and a whole heap
more wisdom than I did!

So there I was, looking for childcare for my now five-
month-old baby, in whose company I had only just really
started to thrive. I 'knew' that I would get a little help from
the government with some sort of tax credit, as many of
my friends had – and I'm talking friends with partners,

so I was sure that as a single mother I would be entitled to some form of help. Turns out, after four interviews at the Job Centre and endless calls to Citizens Advice and some single-parent charities, that because The System was switching over to Universal Credit that month, everything was changing and I wasn't eligible for anything they didn't think, but no one was definitive as the system was 'still new, Miss Thorne'. I had a good salary – not an incredible salary, and definitely not a salary as good as households with two incomes – but a decent salary, and this arbitrary annual figure meant I was not eligible for any financial help in terms of childcare.

I was gutted; I am sure I could have appealed the new (somewhat flawed) system, explored further, but ultimately my time was running out, I was due back at work, which was my own business that I loved and had no intention of leaving, so I had to figure out a way to pay for childcare myself. Avoiding looking into my rights further for fear of being turned away or my ignorance of knowing where to look is truly the definition of my privilege. I knew that somehow I would be able to make it work on my own. I had to. I could cut back. I would have to cut back. I remember at that time thinking about all the vitriol single mothers had received throughout my lifetime for 'cheating and scrounging off the system' – my god, if they had managed to work out a way to cheat the system then all power to them, they deserved every penny for their initiative!

So I remained earnestly searching for childcare. The options seemed to be: a nursery, a childminder, an au pair . . . or magic. To go back to work full-time meant that for a nursery, I was looking at at least £1,000 per month. One. Thousand. Pounds. I'd had a baby, not won the bloody lottery. I was not one of those people who had money put aside at the end of a month either, I was regretfully one of those people who spent everything I had. Either way, there definitely wasn't a 'spare' thousand pounds a month I could whip out of nowhere. So it seemed like nurseries were out of our equation and the best option for me would be to get an au pair.

I lived in Oxford, which was obviously a great place to try to entice people to move to in order for them to look after my child while I worked to earn money to pay them. I had always had lodgers and actually loved the idea of someone else living in the house with me, for company. It would be a great way for Herb to be immersed in other languages, too, depending on where the au pair came from. I would be pretty flexible about their free time because as soon as the working day was covered, they could do what they wanted, have weekends off. I wouldn't expect them to cook or clean as some au pairs were asked to do, so I felt that living with Herb and me could offer someone a really great experience of life in Britain.

I was so excited, envisaging life-long friendships being made, Herb becoming fluent in a language I didn't understand and the three of us becoming a really happy and tight little unit having so much fun that we would all weep when their year came to an end and they had to go home. Also, with an au pair, you offer them lodgings, so the payment in cash they receive is relatively low. One huge stumbling block with my plan, however, was that I worked from home. While this is brilliant in many, many ways, it is not conducive to having a small child around at the same time. My house was also open-plan, and what perhaps could have become an office would need to be the au pair's bedroom, leaving the only space to work being my kitchen table. This had been fine when it was just me and Elvis there; however, it would put huge pressure on the au pair to be out of the house all the time, to make sure that I could get my head down at work and not have work calls interrupted by the screams of a baby wanting to be held by his mother who he could see but wasn't allowed to touch. It just seemed that it would create a really toxic environment for everyone involved instead of the loving, nurturing, exciting atmosphere that I had perfectly envisaged in my head.

I was gutted that I was going to have to let go of another rose-tinted dream, but practicality seemed to suggest that my only option was to find a childminder.

I wrote heartfelt emails to everyone on the list of registered minders I had found on the council website, asking if they had any space and whether they looked after such young babies. A slew of kind but ultimately unhelpful responses filled my inbox. 'Would love to help but I am full', 'Sorry, I don't look after babies that young', 'Have you tried Claire on Elm Road?', 'Maybe ask again nearer the time, I may have some space then.' Even though my return to work could be much more flexible than someone working within the realms of strict HR policies and unempathetic management, I still needed to go back to work, and so this wall of childcare dead-ends was beginning to really panic me. What the fuck had I done? How could I have had a baby and not sorted out childcare first? How could I find an additional £1,000 a month in order to send him to a nursery? Could I try those sex chat lines? I heard you can make great money from them. Or should I see if any of my godparents might be able to help me out with either time or cash? I wasn't sure why they would be inclined to, but at this stage, what choices did I have?

I wished and I wished and I wished for a monetary miracle, for my parents to suddenly appear and proclaim how much they would love to help. I felt trapped by my own self-made circumstances. How do people do this? Scrambling to find solutions, a grave panic rose in me daily. And then, eventually, one day I got an email from a local childminder saying she would love to look after Herb. I hadn't even met her yet but the relief was palpable. The feeling of not being able to gasp for breath already started to dissipate and I could feel things start to settle in my mind. It was all going to be OK. I still had to find around £700 a month, but I would just have to work that out, somehow.

While I admit my ignorance around childcare costs (OK and most things baby related!) was pretty unforgivable, I am also ultimately glad for my bull-in-a-china-shop Taurean nature, because if I had for one minute tried to work out the true financial implications of having a baby alone, with no right to any support from the government, then Herb wouldn't be here now and I can't even contemplate life without him in it. I really recommend looking at the website www.pregnantthen-screwed.com for in depth information about issues that impact pregnant women and working mums.

With a little pep in my step about finding a childmin-der, I eagerly went to meet her and sign the paperwork. I had no idea what I was expecting. I only knew one childminder, with whom I had been on a long jury-duty stretch, and she had been wonderful – caring, compas-sionate and full of tales of days at her allotment with the kids. That was all I knew, so my bar had been set high. I was half expecting a Nanny McPhee and Ma Larkin hybrid who would nurture and nourish my baby and instil him with kindness, warmth and lions and tigers and bears, oh my! Again, I was truly living in a fucking wonderland in my head. Unsurprisingly, the lady I met wasn't from a fairytale, but a very normal, very nice lady who liked kids and had been looking after other people's children for twenty years, since hers were young. Ultimately I chose her because she had a kind face, was less than fifteen miles away (two, in fact!) and was, most importantly, available.

The time came for me to return to work and to hand my son over to someone I had only met for fifteen minutes a couple of weeks before. It was emotionally brutal. I felt so ready to go back to work, to create the life I wanted for Herb, and yet I really couldn't imagine someone else giving him his bottles in the day. Someone else would be looking down at his glinting eyes and his mischievous grin as he merrily slurped down his warm milk, all while I would be at home, with Elvis at my feet, talking to people about their branding needs. It just felt like such a vast new world to try to come to terms with. Another parental side swipe, but this one felt more severe than a swipe, this was a full-on sucker punch, both emotionally and physically. I dreaded the day he would have to start spending time away from me, and yet suddenly (cliché #1034) in the blink of an eye three months had passed and it was Christmas. We had done it, we had completed the first level of being a single, full-time working family. He would go in every day with a smile and leave with a smile, he was such a happy boy. I was so unbelievably relieved and proud. Both Herb and I had slipped easily into our new routine; however, I had this constant nagging sense that this childminder, although lovely, wasn't quite right. Herb had been there three months and they had only left the house twice. When I would pick Herb up, in the late winter afternoon, he would leave the house blinking wildly into the daylight, even though it was almost dark.

Now, while I understand the logistics of taking children out must be a massive kerfuffle, she lived opposite a park and also had a garden she could have just lobbed them into, so they could discover mud and eat worms. Of course, being British and also terrified that she might be mean to Herb if I questioned her about the lack of fresh air and vitamin D that anyone was getting, I said nothing to the childminder and silently maintained the status quo.

I started to look into forest schools as I really think Herb thrives when he is outside lapping up his surroundings and getting mud under his nails. Yet not only was he still too young at that point, it would be cheaper to go on a day trip to Mars than put him in full-time, or even part-time. I'd hit another financial stumbling block. So instead, I began a search for another childminder, one who would teach Herb to get stuck into nature and give him a variety of surroundings to explore. This time the process felt much easier because I had more of an idea of what I was looking for – mainly to find out if they ever ventured outside into the fresh air, or just sat in the dark all day . . . Predictably, as I was in no immediate hurry because I had not given notice to our childminder, I found one straight away. She was absolutely wonderful, she adored Herb and he adored her. She and her family felt like home to us and the love and kindness they nurtured him with was bloody glorious.

My decision to leave the initial childminder was qualified on our last day there. She presented me with a really lovely journal of all the things Herb had done while in her care, including photos and 'drawings' and explanations of his progress. There were also a couple of sticky notes with developmental milestones that he had reached. One of which read:

EAD/PSED

I was sick on the floor. I ran my fingers through it to make a pattern.

For those of you like me, who may not know what those acronyms mean, let me shed some light.

EAD – Expressive Arts and Design.

PSED – Personal, Social and Emotional Development.

Basically meaning that she believed my son playing with his own sick was an artistic expression of his development. Ha! I am not a fussy mother – at all – and Herb spent most of his first two years in a field with his hands in various piles of inexplicable flotsam and jetsam, most of which went into his mouth, but when he was sick, I would tend to clear it up rather than wonder at the beautiful patterns he was creating in it! Like I said, I felt totally vindicated at that moment that I had made the right decision and since then he has had two of the very best childminders in the world. In fact, I am going to be bereft when he ends up going to school and they become less and less part of our daily lives.

THINGS TO THINK ABOUT WHEN CHOOSING A CHILDMINDER:

- Ask what an average day may look like and check that it involves outdoor play.
- Ask how flexible they can be with pick-up times.
- Make sure you are shown around the main play areas in their house.
- Ask where your baby will take their naps.
- Ask the ages of the other children in their care at the moment.
- Ask if you can get 'references' from the other mums. Get their numbers, if possible, because they will be more honest if they are speaking directly to you.
- Find out what their policy on holidays is. How many days do they take a year and will you be charged?

- Do they provide snacks/nappies/wipes, or should you?
- Trust your gut, you will know if it feels right!
- Will they let your child play arts and crafts in their own sick?
- Ask them their favourite booze/treat – they will be looking after the person you love most in the world, you will want to treat them as much as you can by way of a thank-you.
- Talk to them about how they should 'deal with' Father's Day, etc. This could simply be making their favourite uncle/grandad/friend/cousin a card instead. You just want to make sure that your child isn't left to feel the odd one out, that it is all dealt with naturally and kindly.

While the constant juggle of keeping all your balls in the air feels relentless, often magnified when yours are the only hands available to catch said balls, I cannot tell you how truly bloody lucky I feel that I had created a life of flexibility around my work before I had Herb. I had at least had some foresight in one element of my planning for motherhood! One of the many reasons my business partners and I set up our company was because we could see a real need and benefit to working flexibly in terms of hours, holiday days, location, procedures – all of it! Over the last couple of years, there has been a very vocal movement to try to instil flexible working into our job culture. (I would highly recommend you check out Anna Whitehouse's Flex Appeal campaign for in-depth reading about this.) And rightly so, because our system is outdated, deeply flawed and not conducive to having a great work–life balance where both can flourish (not that only those with families need flexibility, literally everyone would benefit). The fact that our standard working day is roughly 9 a.m. to 5.30 p.m. and our standard school day is roughly 8.30 a.m. to 3.30 p.m. shows in black and white the vast chasm of space there is left within which working parents must find childcare solutions. All usually involving yet more money, when often that money can be bloody difficult to find, leaving people in a lose-lose situation and so many women (usually) forced to give up work, when perhaps they may not have wanted to. An archaically rigid system that allows working parents to bluster into the office a little late, flushed of cheek, with a room of eye rolls following them for daring to ensure their kid wasn't left crying in the playground at drop off in favour of making sure they were at their desk at 9 a.m. SHARP. Preferably earlier, to earn bonus points.

I would wager that the irony is, often the fiercest eye-rollers were those with children, but their partner or parents or bank account were enabling them not to have to endure this sort of inexplicable and callous judgement on a daily basis. I can hand on heart say that being in control of my own time and working flexibly with a team (of brilliant men) who have never questioned my commitment or whereabouts is the only reason I can make working full-time, without free childcare help from family, a reality. I honestly cannot imagine a life as a solo mum where I was being clock-watched or reviewed for my time at my desk, rather than the strength of the output of my work and client relationships. Those parents are superheroes. In order to be able to afford childcare without constant worry, I am able to work shorter days and then pick up my work again when Herb is in bed. Obviously this won't be the case forever, but for now, while he is still so young (do not tell me he is nearly three, I won't listen!) and before he starts school when I have to fit in with that timetable (not just the days, I'm talking about those long and inconvenient school holidays when you have to find childcare or camps or who knows what to keep them occupied!), this is a beyond brilliant and frankly mental-health-saving solution that I am intensely grateful for. A flexibility that means so much more to me than money.

I have worked from home for as long as I have had Herb and this arrangement in itself brings its own benefits that make life as a single parent feel a little less strained. I can put a wash on in the day, while still meeting all my deadlines. I can start to cook dinner at lunch time, so when Herb is at home, I can focus on him rather than having to keep him occupied while I chop onions. That said, I have worked really hard with Herb, or indeed without him, on his independent play. It is important to me that while I do want to spend as much time with him as possible, I will also nearly always need to be doing other things too – even just organising the everyday chaos of a middle-of-the-road two-person house and life.

While I absolutely carve out the time to complete life admin when Herb is asleep (if I am not working, of course), I also feel uncomfortable with allowing him to be under the impression there would always be someone there, ready and waiting, to entertain him whenever he should command it. I want us to really enjoy

our time together, to bloom in each other's
company without the pressure of it feeling
forced. Forced may not be the right word,
but ultimately, I don't want him to become
lazy about his own learning. I wanted him,
from a young baby, to explore the world on
his own terms, without props and people
there to pave the way for him. Obviously if he
was unhappy, I was there, but for me it was
absolutely fundamental that he learnt to be
content in his own head, and with his own
discoveries too. I would deliberately leave him
on one side of the room, while I got on with
something on the other. He could see me, he
knew I was there, but I wasn't constantly waving
a toy in his face in order to distract from his
own natural development. I read somewhere
recently that someone wanted their child to
apply their own learnings to things that sparked
their curiosities, rather than be taught how
to pass an exam verbatim, with no fluidity of
applied learning. That is exactly what I want
for Herb, I want him to learn about things that
spark excitement in him, that allow him to stay

up late into the night with a torch under his
duvet avidly reading about his latest obsession.
While I know there has to be some structure to
learning, I am really keen that, where possible,
I would like that to be on his terms, whatever
that may evolve into. I feel so deeply about this
I honestly don't think it is just down to our small
family unit, I think that even if I had twenty-
three children I would feel the same.

The need to give him the space and stimulation to explore
independently, I found really bloody hard. Not wanting
to continue with a tedious treadmill of the same routine,
constantly thinking of things to do with a child who for
a good long while couldn't walk was oddly exhausting,
so work often felt like a welcome relief. I am probably
not supposed to admit that because I wanted a baby for
so long and I should be in a perpetual state of bliss and
never admitting to a moment of hardship or relentless-
ness – blah, blah, blah. I am not that person, though. I
can't sugar-coat it if it is tough, I don't see the point. I
know throughout this journey I have sounded ignorant at
best and privileged at worst, but I truly don't see the need
to pretend anything other than what you are actually

feeling about parenthood, or life in general. Seriously? Who are you trying to kid? If you are loving every second of it, no one sane would begrudge you that at all. Like-wise, if you sometimes fantasise about throwing your kid in the bin or pouring gin in your coffee just to get through the day, then I can pretty much guarantee you aren't alone. So why hide it?

Not only did work feel like a welcome relief some-times, but I also really longed for my own space again sporadically. I had spent my entire adult life in my own company, on my own terms, and no matter how much I was celebrating being a mother, I still yearned to occasionally not have to wake up just because I had no one to pass the baton over to. My sister could totally sense this and from very early on would call, just at the right time, and ask if she could come and get him for a sleepover. She managed to make it feel like I was doing her a favour, because she and her family wanted to spend time with Herb. I know that was true, but I also know she was fully aware that if she pitched it that way it would make me feel easier about asking for help, if I hadn't actually asked at all. Herb absolutely adores my sister and her family, he grins from ear to ear while he is there as they scramble around finding their old toys from the attic for him to play with. They all get on with their day-to-day life, with this added bonus of this little smiley babe in the middle of it and him absolutely lapping up the constant attention he doesn't get from me at home and the illicit treats given to him from their larder.

JUST SOME OF THE TRULY RANDOM THINGS I HAVE LEARNT AS A PARENT:

- Fairy Original Liquid is the absolute queen of stain removal; it will save any shituation.
- Direct sunlight; the free stain-removal alternative to the above!
- Name teddies after the person who gave them to your child – it means not every toy is called Puppy, Bunny or Dino. Also, a crochet pigeon called Maggi, a fawn called Etta and bear called Roe will never not be funny.
- The 'plus' on some nappy sizes does NOT mean bigger. It means more absorbent. Why you would ever want the less-absorbent nappy is beyond me, but who am I to question years of bonkers sizing? They are slightly bigger, but that is apparently not the meaning of the 'plus' symbol.
- Turns out tiny, teeny Tupperware is actually very useful.

- CBeebies Bedtime Stories is absolutely, wholeheartedly created for parental respite . . . Tom Hardy, Josh Homme, Chris Evans, Regé-Jean Page were no accident. Surely Gosling is up next?
- Socks on babies is lunacy, they don't stay on even with specifically created 'sock staying on' inventions. Tights are where it is at. Even boys. In fact, especially boys.
- Babygrows with zips will change your middle-of-the-night nappy changing life. Trust me.
- Absolutely do not panic if a child in your NCT class starts walking at four months and your baby hasn't even learnt to crawl. Unless you think it is due to a genuine problem with their development, then panic not. They will walk, talk, skip, hop, swear back at you in their own sweet time.
- Put the bins out the night before. You can guarantee bin day is the one day the babe will sleep in and you don't want to have to chase the bin lorry down the road with mascara down your face, in old PJs and with leaking nipples.
- Try not to shout at Alexa. I know, this one is hard. However, I found Herb screaming at

her one day, and realised my sister was right when she warned me he would pick up on everything I did. He thinks Alexa is real and that me screaming 'ALEXA, I SAID PLAY *HEY DUGGEE* NOT THE FUCKING GREATEST HITS OF SHAGGY!' at her, made him think this is how you communicate with people! Eeek!

Much like wanting to nurture his independent play, I am also acutely aware that as our family is made up of just two, it could become very easy for either one of us to struggle when we are not in each other's company. So it has always been crucial to me that Herb didn't, where possible, develop a relationship with just me, and be in a situation where no one else was let in or trusted. Going to a childminder as a baby and these overnight stays with my family were an absolute blessing in so many ways, but they were also crucial for him to learn that he could be happy when not in my immediate company, and for both of us to learn to leave each other without anxiety. Now, I'm not going to lie, this mini-holiday arrangement has worked out maybe too well! I am convinced he would rather live with my sister and her doting teenage children and husband who can growl like a tiger.

I find those times apart imperative for my well-being. Don't get me wrong, of course I am that person who stares at photos of her child when they are away, but I'm also revelling in the fact that I am not, for those hours, responsible for him. Those are the sort of things that beautifully illustrate the complex and confusing world of parenthood – you have a dire need for space, but it is a space where you can still constantly see their face! Obviously these overnight breaks weren't weekly or anything, maybe one night every four to six weeks, and while I truly love and need the time to get my shit together every once in a while, it can also exacerbate my loneliness. The push and pull of desperately needing a good stint of sleep, but also wanting to spend time with my friends without a nappy bag outside of my own four walls, and on top of that, longing to see Herb's relationship with my sister blossom before my very eyes. That is just one of the emotional juggles of parenting that everyone speaks of. Every parent has it, I can't say whether it is more raw for those of us doing it alone, but it sometimes feels like it from this side of the fence. The bowers of single-parent life all too often spiked with thorns. My advice to every mother out there: take the help when offered it by someone you trust to take good care of your child; it's good for you, good for them, and good for your relationship with them too.

THINGS YOU CAN DO WHEN OTHER PEOPLE ARE BABYSITTING YOUR CHILD

(N.B.: don't feel obliged to make sure you Have Plans, sometimes you truly just need time to yourself to get your shit together again.)

- Go to the cinema in the afternoon – is there a greater joy in the world?
- Go for a walk at sunset – either with or without friends.
- Go out for dinner – I can't do 2 a.m. finishes anymore because I will never have the time to recover, but a great dinner with friends and bed by 10.30 p.m. is The Dream.
- Get a takeaway, that you collect. After dark. Wild!
- Go to bed at 4 p.m. and feel in no way guilty about it.
- Nip out. Doesn't matter where to, just nip there. Nip to the garage with just your keys and a purse solely to get a magazine. Bliss.
- Wear white.

Developmental leaps aside, there is always a new dynamic to adjust to, and none more so than in 2020 – for me, it was not just the pandemic hitting, but everything that led up to it. There were a couple of months in 2019 when Herb and I just weren't getting on. He was at the stage where he so desperately wanted to communicate, but he just couldn't. He had a low-level whinge that ran round my brain for a couple of months. It totally infiltrated my soul. We were both so frustrated and my fuse got shorter and shorter – obviously not ever to a level that was dangerous for Herb, but it was pretty dangerous for my mental health. It felt like nothing I did was right, he just wasn't happy.

I have to concede that I believe the reason I found it so hard is because I had been so very bloody lucky with him up until that point. Herb was a really happy, really content baby. I was so fortunate that he never had colic, or teethed too badly, he had always loved his sleep as soon as he was in a routine, I had never really had to work through any truly bad experiences with him, other than the day-to-day norm of a happy, healthy baby. Sure, there were some days that were tough and some of those developmental leaps felt like they would break me, but at his core he was your stereotypical bundle of pure joy. I was honestly so beyond lucky. I think that because I had been so shellshocked by the first three months, I had assumed that I was always going to feel like a hollow version of my former self. Then it seemed that every day after that, it started to feel, not effortless so much, but definitely less like wing-walking. So when I felt like I had finally reached a stage where the side swipes weren't going to come so thick and fast, this sudden overnight switch in him felt brutal. I didn't think I was ever going to feel as disconnected as I did in the early days, yet here I was, over a year later, and I could feel those acutely desolate feelings returning.

Every day felt truly relentless, literally nothing would make him happy. Oddly, he would smile a lot still, but he would be smiling while whingeing. The noise and the desperation was chipping away at me, I would shout at him, he would scream at me, then we would hug each other, both crying. Yet still the daily clashes continued. There were times when my sisters could tell I was at breaking point and would arrange to have him scooped up and taken away from me, just to give me a breather. It was those times that the thought of having someone to share the load with sounded like heaven. I would have put up with almost any of the really shitty parts of a relationship in exchange for not being woken up by low-level moaning, or to be able to hand over the baby and just go out for a walk to remind myself how much I loved him and that nothing he was doing was a personal attack on my abilities as a mother. Herb being unhappy wasn't him pointing out my flaws, he wasn't cross with me, he was cross with not being able to communicate and yet I found it almost impossible not to feel like he was just trying to tell me I was a shit mum.

This carried on for what felt like years, but it was just a couple of months, and soon the whingeing dissipated just as quickly as it had arrived. Suddenly Herb's giggle was back, the hugs felt abundant with love rather than despair and the limitless glory of our relationship returned with gumption. Then, March 2020 hit. I say this with all sincerity, if Herb and I had been in lockdown together those few months earlier, I am not sure we would have both survived. While the feeling of being trapped in an odd sci-fi film that I would never have chosen to watch was uniquely scary, nothing would have been scarier than locking Herb and me away together in those latter months of 2019.

As I write this, the UK is emerging slowly from its third lockdown and little could have prepared me, or any other (solo) parent, for the intensity and desperation of this last year. I was ultimately hugely lucky, but

I really had to keep reminding myself of that, almost in some form of daily mantra. I had a roof over my head, my job was, unbelievably, largely unaffected, I wasn't living in fear, my family and friends were healthy and I had access to the most glorious green space with animals to stroke and rivers to paddle in. Yet I was alone with my one-year-old child, trying to do a full-time job, having also just agreed to write a book, and in the middle of selling the house that I had loved so very much for ten years, because fertility treatment, childcare and a very real inability to control my finances had left me in a debt that only selling my house could get me out of.

I had genuine fear that our life was just about to implode, and the main reason I 'got through' lockdown was because my village community was brilliant. So the thought of moving somewhere I didn't know, at a time when you couldn't really easily meet people, felt startling. The pressure of it all seemed totally insurmountable. As ever, my wonderful sister swooped in. She and her family had discussed it and they had happily agreed that they would look after Herb every other weekend, as if we were a family that had two parents sharing joint custody. I felt the weight slowly but surely lift throughout my whole soul when she called me to offer this help, like a too-full balloon being given a slow puncture, an absolute, palpable release.

So, just like we had when Herb was just a few weeks old, we met in a car park halfway between our houses, this time having driven through deserted roads, and I put all his things on the floor of the car park, while she took Herb and we danced around each other in masks, making sure there was at least two metres between us at all times. It felt desperate. I so badly needed her to hug me, but we truly didn't want to break any rules.

As she drove away and left me in the car park, that first time we 'met' in lockdown, my old car that hadn't been used for a few weeks just wouldn't start. I was stranded, alone, in a deserted car park in what felt like the apocalypse. Hot, violent tears poured down my face. I just wanted someone to hold me. The RAC man was very lucky he didn't get me clinging onto his leg when he arrived a record twenty minutes later because their brilliant call centre had been so worried about my wellbeing due to my breathless, pathetic SOS call to them.

That was sort of the start of a mild breakdown that I had, possibly along with much of the country, due to the pandemic and the sum of all its parts. It was such an extreme time. My amazing friends and family would look after Herb so that I could carve time around my job to write this book. That in itself felt like a double-edged sword. While I feel like I have a story to tell in order to try to normalise the idea of donor families, I am not a natural writer and the need to write at very specific times I found actually quite debilitating.

I think much of it was that I was also in desperate need of company. I had spent most of the year alone with my son and/or working, so when friends and family would look after Herb to afford me the time to write when lockdown restrictions would allow, it came at the price of me not being able to spend time with them too, so in essence I would be alone again. Did I make banana bread? Are you kidding? The only thing I made was a call to the doctor to ask for prescribed help. We moved house, twice. We moved childminders, twice. I kept working full-time and I wrote a book. I am assuming nothing will ever feel as hard, isolated, terrifying, intense, solitary, amplified, flawed, angry, trapped or oddly mundane as 2020. So, apologies if the release of this book is a little later than anticipated, it took me a while to get my head into gear around the moving boxes and face masks!

When it all started, my boy was just one, barely talking, and now we are on the precipice of our third move to a beautiful new home in a third lockdown and he is just about to turn three and could talk the tiny front arms off a T-Rex. I don't know how,* but we made it through. I doubt that will be the last time we make it through some rough times together, either, and I am acutely grateful I am able to do it all with him and his big grin by my side.

(*OK sure, so I do know how we made it through. We did it with a constant – and I mean constant – stream of carb deliveries as I still wasn't drinking at home alone for fear of being knee-deep in gin by 11 a.m.!)

CHAPTER 8:
SINGLE, SOLO,
JUST MUM

I suspect that there is a lot of crossover when you are finding your feet as a new parent whether you are single or not. It is funny, since deciding to actually go it alone to become a mum, the difference between the feelings I harboured about what I thought would be difficult versus what I have actually found difficult now that it's my reality, is blooming colossal. I couldn't even put a finger on exactly what it is, or give you specific examples, because there is literally something that will happen almost daily that I hadn't ever even considered. What I can confirm is the learning curve has been steep and fast and very fucking real. There is no course you can go on when your baby is born to tell you exactly what to do – no handbook, no certificate, no right answer. What there is, however, is a lot of generous but subjective advice, a couple of books you may find you relate well to, a colourful array of filtered realities and a massive dollop of good, old-fashioned, everyday judgement. There is also the sudden and overwhelming feeling that you have joined some form of club that has an initiation ceremony that would make most university rugby team inductions feel like a spa day.

Like I said, on the perimeter, whether you are doing it alone or as part of a team, the Good Ship Motherhood will leave you grappling for a life jacket pretty early on. Yet once you have got over the initial shock of being immersed in its freezing waters, you find you can doggy paddle around quite nicely for a while, before treading water again and, occasionally, just occasionally, you feel like just your arm is above the water and you are flailing around calling for help. I can assure you if it really was like swimming in open water, I would have drowned. I can also promise you wouldn't be the only parent out there gasping for breath, despite the images of blissful motherhood you might think you see around you.

Where my reality may differ to what is, possibly unfairly, considered 'the norm' is twofold, in that I am both a single mother by choice and an old mother. Only one of those words makes me roll my eyes – and it isn't 'single'! I have grown up in a world where there is such a huge strain put on the word 'single' when it comes to motherhood. Our beloved British press love nothing more than to paint a picture of single mothers as lazy, uneducated money grabbers. There is a very real narrative of shame when it comes to single mothers in Britain – possibly globally but I can't say. I do know that it wasn't long ago that single mothers would be sent away to asylums to have their children in secret, with assumptions being made that becoming pregnant was an immoral mistake that should be hidden away and forgotten about. Yet here I was, only a couple of decades later, making a very informed, assured decision to have a child alone, without so much as an illicit out-of-wedlock romp for people to gossip about. Perhaps that is why there is such a strong reaction to the word 'solo' being used to describe the parenting situation of people who have knowingly decided to get pregnant by way of a donor as a single person.

Obviously, I think it is actually much more complicated and layered than the difference between a single and a lone or solo mother, but for me, I am proud to be called either. I focus far more on the power of the word 'mother' than any adjective before it. I am acutely aware that for me to be able to proudly make that choice to become a 'solo' parent was, again, a very privileged one, one that is often not afforded to those who are labelled 'single' mothers, when very often their singleness is not something that was their choice, or what they would have perhaps planned. It is a very nuanced and heated discussion, but from my viewpoint, I can assure you I have never come across a single or solo parent that is lazy or entitled; more usually they have a fire in their belly and a fierce craving to carve a life of abundance for their kids. I have never felt ostracised or outcast for being a single/solo parent and my god I am so bloody grateful for that, as I cannot imagine how it would feel to be demonised for simply raising, loving and wanting the very best for my child without the inexplicable and historic glare of strangers wishing to scrutinise me and my every action.

THREE THINGS TO SAY AT PARTIES TO STOP PEOPLE ASKING STUPID QUESTIONS:

- Oh, his dad? I have absolutely no idea who he is.
- Yeah, he is cute, thanks. I paid good money for him.
- There is a great four-year, money-back guarantee, so I could still send him back.

The fundamental difference between single and lone/solo parenting is that of shared responsibility. I cannot describe this without making some very generalised observations; I don't mean these to be defamatory or to describe whole sections of society as very 2-D beings, but I need to start this way in order to illustrate my own personal realities! This entire book, in fact our whole lives, is made up of spectrums, of caveats, of edge cases, and I cannot even begin to cover all of those when it comes to parenthood, especially as I only know how it has been for me, from my subjective vantage point.

When it comes to responsibility, though, that is a very real thing in terms of solo parenting, and as always it comes wrapped in swathes of both positive and negative emotions. Absolutely everything that happens to Herb stems, in some way, from a decision or a choice that I have to make alone. That can go from the very mundane decisions about what socks I should buy him, to much more life-shaping and epic debates about who should I ask to be his guardian should anything happen to me? You see, he has no back-up plan, I am all he has, legally speaking.

Then, of course, there is every other life-shaping decision in between: when should I potty train him, when do I start taking him to the dentist, how do I instil kindness in him, how do I start to teach him about the complexities and injustices of race, how do I not pass on any of my anxieties to him? Can I make sure he likes spiders when they make me jump out of my skin, what clothes should I buy him, what sort of diet should he have, am I happy for him to have swimming lessons from a few months old, how can I infuse the magic of Christmas into his very soul without him thinking Father Christmas is a creepy old man? And it doesn't stop there, I have to decide how I can save for him to go to university if he wants to, should I enrol him in something like cubs or do I want something more unisex – or is unisex an outdated word now? What life insurance should I have for us, how can I ensure he knows he is so very loved, how on earth will I teach him his times tables, when should I introduce him to technology, is my pension going to be enough, how will I teach him how to really love himself, how can I encourage his passions, how will I explain the earth is round, how can I stop him picking his nose, how can I soothe him after a fall?

All of this and so much more. So much more. Literally everything. Everything is down to me. They are all my decisions, to make alone, on his behalf. Of course I can ask for advice, or go with the general consensus after a straw poll from fellow mothers and friends, but ultimately the final decision is down to me (and sometimes him!) and that can feel very heavy and often pretty lonely. The worst part is that 98 per cent of the time, there is no right answer either. Sure, you can do your best to educate yourself to make informed decisions and decisions you are comfortable with, but ultimately he is a person with his own psyche and mind and beliefs and I just have to do my very best to nurture and guide him.

Honestly, it is mainly the big things like ensuring he knows to love fiercely, to harbour his passions, to live limitlessly, that I worry I will fail at alone. Some of this may be innate, some of this he will learn from friends and family, so it isn't really, truly, solely down to me, I know. What is down to me is doing the laundry, taking the bins out, making sure he is well fed, plying him with suncream, renewing the car insurance – all the day-to-day crap that ensures our little piece of the world still turns. The flip side of the sole responsibility of this mundanity is that I know that I have to do it. I know it is me and me alone who will make sure we are wearing clean clothes, that there is milk in the fridge for his bottles, that the mortgage gets paid, that Herb gets into bed, that the dog gets fed, that the dishwasher gets unloaded. Me. Myself. I. There is no one to harbour resentment towards. I will not be unloading the dishwasher at night, having cooked for Herb and put him to bed, thinking, 'Fucking hell, Dave is late from work again, it was his turn to unload the washer because I did the cooking and he hasn't seen Herb for two days.' And on and on the spiral goes.

I have no Dave. Dave is not going to put the bins out. Dave is not going to save me in the middle of the night if I hear a noise downstairs. Dave is not going on his twelfth stag do this year, leaving me home alone with Herb, having asked his interfering mother to check in on us. Dave didn't say he would pick Herb up from school but forgot. Dave won't be arranging the insurance. Dave won't offer his opinion on which school Herb should go to. Dave isn't going to hang the washing out. Dave isn't going to teach Herb to climb a tree. Dave doesn't exist. I am Dave. I have to do it all and I can hold no negative feelings about that because there is no one else that 'should' be doing those things. Just me. I made this decision. Me. Sometimes I think that this lack of dependency on others is far easier than the feeling of being let down by someone you are supposed to be in parental cahoots with.

While I see this is an unexpected advantage of solo parenting, where one huge disadvantage comes in, is financially. This is also where there can be the widest gap between a solo parent and a single parent. Again, there are spectrums and caveats, but I have to generalise to make the point. Very often single parents will have some form of financial help from the other parent. Mind you, the spectrum of that alone can also be vast – anything from ensuring their child never wants for anything to having to beg for the other parent to contribute towards school uniforms. Thus the vicious circle of resentment creeps in again, but it is one that a solo parent simply won't have as there is no one to resent for not fully committing to the financial and emotional wellbeing of the child. That is not to say that the financial burden on a solo parent isn't epic – believe me, it truly is – but knowing it is all down to you can be just as liberating as it is constraining.

A solo parent also doesn't ever have to compromise their beliefs or have their rules undermined by the other parent. The all-too-familiar '. . . but Mum/Dad said I could' narrative won't happen in our house. Herb will know the rules, our rules, and there will be no one who can swoop in later without the deep frustrations of a mundane parenting day and sabotage any consequences that I had set in place.

It is all swings and roundabouts. Parenting is extreme in its implications, no matter who or how many people are doing it. It is unique for all of us and perhaps that is why there seems to be a fierce need for your particular strand of parenting to be labelled correctly. Solo, single, separated, joint, absent, widowed – these are all descriptors that afford other people looking in the ability to try to understand the realities of your personal parental situation. You are not a single parent if your loving husband works away for parts of the year and leaves you at home; you are a parent who is looking after your kids without help while your partner earns money for your family, but who can still check in, help with decisions and ease some of the burden. Those are the sort of flippant comments from other parents that can make truly single, solo parents take a sharp intake of breath. Much like bonkers phrases such as 'daddy day care'. Are you kidding me? This isn't day care, this is simply a man looking after his own children! It is not, or at least shouldn't be, an event to be documented!

TERMS LIKELY TO CAUSE THE BIGGEST MARMITE REACTION IN THE DONOR MUM COMMUNITY:

- Single mum versus solo mum.
- Diblings (donor siblings).
- Donor versus dad.
- Open donors versus anonymous donors (within the realms of the law).
- Social media donors.
- The phrase 'turkey basting'.

So, I truly don't care if you call me a single or a solo mum, but call me old and I will be hard pushed not to give you a wedgie. I think the age at which you become geriatric in terms of fertility is thirty-five. Thirty-five! I still can't quite believe how outdated that seems. Sure, there are stats that prove your fertility chances start to dip considerably the older you get, but a) you don't need to go straight to the word geriatric, b) your internal organs don't implode at midnight on your thirty-fifth birthday like a Fertility Cinderella and c) fuck off.

Apart from the age of your reproductive organs, I find the obsession with maternal age quite bizarre. Young mothers are absolutely vilified in this country and belittled, judged, ignored. Heaven help them if they are young *and* *gasp* single. The inexplicable misogyny that is so often woven through these blanket judgements of young mothers is quite bizarre to me, as someone who has never had to experience it, especially not at my most vulnerable. There is rarely the expectation that a young mum, especially a teenage one, will thrive. Yet my immediate reaction to young mothers is quite the opposite of the vitriol they can be used to, it is, in fact, jealousy. Again, I say this as someone who has never experienced being ostracised for being a young mother, but I am deeply jealous of how much more time they are likely to be able to spend with their children in terms of life span. Yes, again, there are always caveats and people may die young or other tragedies may befall them, as I well know, but I am blinded by the fact they are likely to be able to spend at least fifteen years more with their kid than I will with Herb. I cannot believe what judgement they are put under for having children at an age that is not deemed acceptable by the Acceptable Police. My mum had her first child at seventeen and died when she was fifty. The rhythms of life beat very differently for everyone and I cannot understand why it is anything other than the business of those involved and their own reproductive system. Let alone the bloody peculiar twist of first-time mums in their thirties giving patronising advice to first-time teenage mums, as if they know any better because they have waited until a 'more suitable' age. I am convinced that it doesn't matter what age you are, you know a little less than zero about parenting until you have actually lived through its unbridled clutches.

Which leads me to why I hate being called an 'Old Mum'. I am choosing to ignore the phrase geriatric; mainly because I am just not sure what it has to do with anything at all. I was three weeks away from my thirty-ninth birthday when I gave birth, so my tits were nearing my ankles before I even tried (and failed) to have Herb nourished by them. It is assumed by other people that I am a Big Serious Career Woman who deliberately 'put my life on hold' to try to rule the corporate world before I decided to let a little tiny baby me enter the world. As it happens, I do love my job, but does it have anything to do with me being a mother in my late thirties? Absolutely not. Is it the fact that people think I have a career, that is presumed more acceptable, more stable, for me to have had a child later than it would have been if I had been a careerless teen? Like I say, the blanket judgement and assumptions that are created around motherhood in all her glory I find inconsequential and fucking dull.

Call me old if you think I am old, but don't call me old because of when I managed to bear fruit from my loins. It is also wildly scaremongering for those women who would love children, are in their early thirties, single and have their mother screaming down the Easter table that she read in the *Daily Mail* that 'if you weren't pregnant by 25.7, you may as well forget it'. Women know the complexities of the biological clock, they live through it every fucking month, what they don't need is a cacophony of clarion calls about it. It is exhausting. In the same way that teen mothers are surely exhausted by consistently being represented as unable to possibly know how to look after a baby. I am thrilled for those who managed to find love, buy a house, get married and have their first child by twenty-five (although this prime age changes annually, of course, *eye roll*) without any fertility issues so that they don't have to bear witness to the constant scrutiny of those who dared to have children before or after that point, but for the rest of us, I plead with you to just stop the constant narrative about timing perfection.

That is not to say that, for me, there haven't been some advantages to having children later than my friends. I have had the pleasure of being able to watch them learn as parents from the sidelines. To accidentally pick up titbits of information that have helped me feel more confident about being a mother myself. It's an advantage of having a baby after them, but that's not down to the age that I became a mother – it could have been that all my friends had children at twenty-five and I learnt all of these gems of information before I was thirty. It just happens that my friends started having babies in their early twenties and carried on until their late thirties and I have been there throughout.

Receiving the benefit of their experience means that certain aspects of motherhood that I may have worried about should I not have been around parents of young children for most of my adult life, no longer felt like anything I should be concerned about as long as I was comfortable with my decision and my baby was happy and healthy.

First up on the list is that milky hot potato of breast-feeding. I have witnessed the full and wonderful gamut of passionate highs and despairing lows that being able to feed your own child from your own body can bring. It truly is a miraculous and awesome gift of nature. It is also one that comes with the most monumental amount of crushing pressure. There is a period of time after birth when it is all that people can talk about. Has your milk come in? Is he latching? Did you catch the colostrum? Do cabbage leaves really soothe the pain? When can I start expressing? The questions and thoughts go on and on. What no one will really prepare you for, however, is the looks of sharp disappointment and sheer disillusionment you will receive if you state that you are no longer breastfeeding. Truth is, between Herb physically pulling away whenever I drew him close for a feed, the fact that my milk never really came and many, many things in between, I never truly breastfed. My boy was raised on bottles of formula and he and I are totally, completely and fully content with how that journey worked out for us.

I am very much part of the 'fed is best' camp and, like much of motherhood, I can't see why, how one person chooses with insight to do something, it should ignite such vitriol in those who have nothing to do with either mother or child who take the opposite opinion. It seems to be a deeply flawed metric to me, and one that allows mothers to pit themselves against each other, which can only ever be harmful. I longed to breastfeed my child, yet having seen many friends struggle as well as those who flourished, I knew I would do what I felt was right when my time came.

Which is exactly what I did. Thankfully, my midwife didn't make a scene when we made the decision on day seven or eight, she didn't belittle or force me, she gently held my hand and explained what she knew about formula feeding. I think, had I not been privy to so many friends' journeys with feeding, I may have felt pressured to do something that absolutely wasn't working for us physically or mentally, and I am so very grateful that those who mattered never once made me feel anything other than informed to help me decide to do what was right for me and my son.

This is just one example of experiences and decisions that I now think, with a little life in my sails and having lived through the parental experiences of others, have made me profoundly comfortable with doing what feels best for me and for Herb, and I truly give no shits about what others who have nothing to do with me want to project onto me. As I get to grips with the unique chaos of becoming a mum, I am grateful that I am so very at peace with the parenting decisions I have made so far. I can't do everything 'by the (fictional) book', all the time – and nor would I want to, because we will make mistakes together. I will make mistakes as a solo parent, no matter how much I read, observe and learn. Yet I am so assured that my sheer passion to be the best person I can be for Herb is going to get us through, kicking and screaming!

There are more mundane things that I am totally relaxed about, too. Driving with Herb, for example. I know so many parents who sit in the back of the car with their child while their partner drives. What the bloody hell am I supposed to do in that situation? Seriously? There would have been a time that I would have worried that me not holding his hand or checking he was breathing correctly or singing to his face would have meant that I wasn't looking after him properly. That I wasn't nurturing him enough. Yet I soon realised that people did this because their circumstance afforded them to be able to; they probably wanted to be near their babe, rather than the babe needing them nearby. No judgement either way, because I think you become accustomed to what you are able to offer your child at the time. Fact is, in a car, I can't offer Herb anything! I didn't even get one of those mirror things you hang on the back of the seat of the car. I could never imagine a time when I would feel safe driving over two tons of car, looking through a mirror, into a mirror, to see if the mottled reflection would give me any indication of him being discontent. I decided if he was really unhappy, I would hear him. I would stop, I would sort it. And now,

Herb is very used to just being totally ignored in the car as he wistfully looks out of the window counting trees or proclaiming to see tigers. This is neither a good nor a bad thing, it is just what worked for us and what we have become used to. Likewise, when his first jabs came around, friends of mine would go together with their partner and their baby, which initially made me question whether I should ask one of my sisters to come with me. Again, both the parents went to the jab because they both wanted to, not because they *needed* to. Of course, Herb was absolutely fine with it just being me who went with him, as fundamentally that is all he knew. It is me and him. Him and me.

That's not to say that I found these things out – and more! – without some elements of trial and error along the way. There were certain parts of being Herb's mum that absolutely floored me. I have a deep and complicated relationship with his pram, for example. Holy shit, they are so big and so complicated! As stupid as it sounds, I really wish I had practised with it before Herb arrived rather than scrambling around with the bloody levers and clicky bits and hoods and straps while clutching a wailing newborn in my hot, sweaty arms. One of the first times I left the house alone with Herb, I really felt like A Mum. I had got together all

the crap we could ever possibly need and a shedload
of stuff we didn't – two changes of clothes, nappies,
wipes, bottles, Calpol, Infacol, muslins, padded suit,
blankets, a teddy, a crinkly book, a pram rain cover,
gloves, a hat, Sudocrem, arnica, Papaw ointment, suncream – literally everything, just to get in the car to
drive four minutes up the road to try to get a coffee
from M&S. I just wanted to get out with him somewhere familiar, to prove to myself that I could do it,
that we would be OK, especially as I had packed my
trendy nappy bag with All The Things, so I wouldn't
look like that person who didn't know what they were
doing. Reader, I didn't know what I was doing.

About three hours after I first decided to leave
the house, I got to the outdoor car park and excitedly went to the boot to get the pram out to go and
peacock around M&S with my beautiful baby boy.
What actually happened was that I tried and I tried
and I tried to open the buggy contraption until I
was left in a sobbing, soggy heap on the filthy con-
crete floor of the car park, emotionally ravaged by
a bastard buggy. I remember the fast spiral of emotions from excitement to despair. A man walked by
and asked if I was OK, I said I would be fine, and he
insisted he would come back and check on me in a

few minutes, clearly sensing my fake proclamations of OKness. He was obviously not new to seeing the emotional intensity of a young mother just trying to get through the day. I wondered how many children he had. I have no idea if he did come back and check, because once I had retrieved the Bastard Buggy from where I had thrown it, I slung it back in the boot and skulked home, totally bereft and coffeeless. It took me a few more months to realise that the Bastard Buggy was the worst contraption to ever grace the earth, and instead of trawling Facebook marketplace again for a suitable replacement, I went straight to buy a new one that flipped open with one swift, beautiful, hassle-free move, by way of my bulging credit card. Never was I going to be defeated by a buggy again.

I don't believe in guilt as a general rule (especially 'guilty pleasures', why on earth should you feel guilty about something that brings you pleasure?) and I definitely don't subscribe to the notion of 'Mum guilt'. These are things that I think I am supposed to feel guilt about. I don't. Neither should you.

- Having to go to work.
- Herb still being in nappies aged three.
- Herb still having bottles aged three.
- Herb still being in a cot aged three (he's contained for fourteen hours a day, it's perfect!).
- Herb watching films so I can get some peace (if you are in the newborn fog, please know that one day, not too far off, your baby will be able to watch a film all the way through and it will be glorious).
- Herb not having any technology aged three.
- Herb not having a bath every day (he didn't have one for a year at one stage because he decided he was scared, so 'only' having around four a week feels like a luxury).
- Having never washed Herb's hair.
- Feeding Herb beige shop-bought food sometimes.
- Not reading to him every night if one of us is too tired.
- Shouting at Herb.
- Not being a skivvy to housework.
- Not taking him on wild, expensive adventures, every single weekend.
- Herb having no grandparents.

- Not making motherhood a competition of who has it hardest/best.
- Longing to feel #blessed but actually feeling #fuckingtired.
- Shopping for him in the girls' section.
- Not enjoying motherhood every. Single. Second.
- Yearning to thrive but sometimes barely surviving.
- Not being able to give Herb a sibling.
- Not picking Herb up every time he cries.
- Embarrassing Herb – that is his birth right and my right as his mother!

If I have to, I can chuck the credit card at many problems – like buggies that don't make me weep (although now I have cut up my cards, this is now a bit trickier!) , but the heavy feelings of loneliness that come with being a parent on your own can be crippling and can't be so easily solved. Of course, you absolutely aren't alone, as there is a small human nearly always within a couple of metres of you, but that doesn't negate the feelings of loneliness that can totally blanket you every day. Very often I found my usual set of friends could be at work, college or doing the school run at the time when I needed to be out of my own four walls in the quest for company. So I forced myself to join the local mother and baby groups in the pursuit of other adults with whom I hoped to have a normal conversation, or who at least could respond to me! There I discovered that the loneliness I was feeling may also be true for parents who are in relationships, as this can be the only reasonable explanation for the crippling awkwardness of a baby group that you have unwillingly gone to in order to meet other mums (or because your darling sisters insisted you should go)!

Despite my desperate need for community, for a chat with others about whether it was normal for your baby to be shitting green liquid, I felt absolutely, excruciatingly uneasy sitting in on these groups. I walked into the sessions as a middle-class white woman with a healthy neuro-typical kid, but I cannot imagine the isolation that I would have felt if that weren't the case. So often these groups met in some non-accessible library or village hall that smelt of both must and damp. You loitered around, trying to catch the eye of someone you thought, on fleeting, sleep-deprived first impressions, looked like they might be struggling with motherhood just as much as you were. What you didn't want was to be sat next to the person who had brushed their hair recently, was wearing clean white jeans and whose baby had no clear signs of snot on their face. Those mothers had their shit together, or, worse, knew how to pretend they had their shit together!

This has been another lesson in motherhood for me. You are repeatedly forced into situations with people just because you have had children at the same time, but often all you have in common *is* the children. Suddenly it is all you can talk about. You literally have no chat left. You are just talking in circles about sleep patterns, routines, how to get stains out of clothes and the best nappy rash cream. Or, worse, the weather. These groups weren't for me – at all – it was like organised fun while seeking out Breton-striped, Converse-wearing (both things I own, FYI, no shade!) women who had also recently squeezed a kid out.

Ironically, what I did find helpful was the hyped-up version of the simple local baby group: Instagram. I don't know if it is because you already followed each other, so it didn't feel so much like you were meeting strangers – even though you clearly were – but meeting up with local mums I met on Instagram became an absolute tonic, a total lifeline. When you are home alone with a baby 24/7, the thought of being outside in a park with other people you get on with may as well be a lottery win. The only sense of sadness comes when you all leave; I knew they were going home and at some point that day they would see another adult, feel the touch of another adult. Yet I was sloping off back home alone and it could be up to three days before I would see another adult again.

Being lonely is pretty desolate, but making plans to see people to alleviate that loneliness could often feel like a military operation in order to get it to fit around schedules. Keeping my mind ticking along in those early days felt hard, when it could be day after day of just Herb for company, sat opposite him in a coffee shop, walking him through the meadow, endless time-consuming supermarket trips, inexplicable outings to garden centres even though my hatred of gardening runs deep. That is not to say Herb wasn't great company, of course, but there is only so much gurgling and hoping farts were smiles that you could find entertaining, even if totally beguiling. Online chatter about 'must-see' TV series makes you feel like you aren't totally disconnected from the world, like you are watching it with friends. A strange sort of fictional camaraderie. Another thread to desperately pull through the ever-tightening eye of the needle that was once my sense of self.

CELEBRATE THE EVERYDAY (DON'T PUKE – I MEAN IT!)

- Write down the little things that happen, even if they seem mundane. You won't regret it because your memory will fade. (I have recently found an amazing journal, that you fill in monthly for eighteen years! Being every month not every day means I am much more likely to fill it in. It is called the Childhood Journal, by Month of Sundays.)

- Lean into the repetitive – kids love, absolutely love, repetition. So rather than get frustrated, try to relish the fact that you are listening to Elton John's 'I'm Still Standing' for the fourteenth time that day. One day they won't even want to be in the same room as you, let alone dance while you play air piano.

- Embrace the fact that life isn't all peachy and Instagram filtered. If your kid has an enormous loud and smelly poo on the bus, don't fret. Laugh it off. Everyone shits. People will get over it. You aren't failing.

- Follow your child when they wander through a wood, don't dictate the route. It's fascinating to see what piques their interest and what decisions they make when you aren't leading them.

- Your child will fall down. They will also learn to get back up again. Let them. Nine times out of ten, it is hilarious to witness!
- Let the dog clean under the high chair. No one is looking.
- Just watch. Preferably if they don't realise you are doing so. Kids are captivating.

The mundane beauty of those days have, sadly, rarely been documented photographically with me in the frame alongside Herb. You see, when you live alone with a baby, there is only you to take the photos. So your camera roll is solely of the baby, the baby and the dog, a screenshot from your phone of useful advice, the occasional really shit selfie, but never just a natural shot of you and your baby caught off guard. There are moments you wish you could bottle – the first laugh, proper guttural laughs that allow you to really celebrate the magic of the world you have created. You have to keep your wits about you to make sure that these raw, connected, beautiful moments of a tiny hand wrapped around your finger or of the first time you know, really know, that they have recognised you don't get swallowed up by the more humble mundanity of early parenthood. The beauty is there, it really, truly is, it is just sometimes hard to see it through the fact that you have just put on the same load of washing for the third time. Yet the pride you feel at the end of another long day of parenting solo, as you put your babe down to sleep, is like the best form of natural high. We did it again, kid, we thrived another day!

CHAPTER 9: CHOOSE YOUR OWN ADVENTURE

So, here I am, the solo mum of a brilliant boy who is just about to turn three. Cliché #2875, time really does slip through your fingers when you see it through a child's eyes. Looking back at that tiny, red, ET-esque squirmy worm that I paid to have grown in my belly, I simply cannot fathom that he is the handsome, cheeky, kind, raucous, happy, hairy, kerfuffle monkey that I am lucky enough to call my own. Christ alive, it has felt so very hard, there have been moments when I didn't think we could possibly make it, then add just a soupçon of a global pandemic into the mix and it feels vaguely miraculous that we are both here to tell the tale, both still smiling. A tale that, if it were down to Herb, would be a prehistoric one punctuated with fart jokes and the occasional inexplicable giraffe.

So as I look back on the past three years, is it what I had expected? Is it everything I had dreamt of? Well, as you can imagine, that isn't an easy question to answer. Motherhood has this quite extraordinary ability to strip you bare, to make you see things about yourself that you had never been privy to before. Extraordinary things, too, like your ability to triumph, the visceral love that you feel not only for your child but for your family and friends, the intense connection you create within yourself in order to realise how you want to encourage your child to flourish and the soft healing that giving yourself completely to someone else can bring.

Motherhood has made me understand the reason why these clichés exist and why there is no handbook for parenthood. No one can write a handbook for something that simply cannot be explained. Sure, there can be books like this that offer a tiny peep into a personal perspective, but there is nothing that can give an explanation to the raw depth of feeling that becoming a parent leaves within you. There are vast spectrums of feelings bandied around everywhere – from feeling trapped, to ragged with tiredness, to basking in the absolute, sheer, bloody glory of it all.

I think maybe the best description is bonkers. Bonkers good. Bonkers bad. Bonkers mundane. Bonkers brilliant. So perhaps that is why, when I am asked by people if I would 'recommend' solo motherhood, I cannot possibly answer. After all, you are talking about creating human life and all that comes with it. I wouldn't even encourage people to get a dog (OK, I would, they are wonderful, you won't regret it) let alone have the audacity to tell them whether I feel they should have a child, or what age I think the best time to start having a child is, or how much fertility treatment costs. These are seriously open-ended questions that come with iceberg-like responses that you could answer subjectively, but beneath the surface of these is a ten-ton solid mass of implication and consideration that you may or may not be prepared for. What I can tell you is that I have tried to point out the more difficult parts of parenting alone, those things that I didn't necessarily anticipate, because I feel that the joys of parenting don't have to be pointed out as they feel so very obvious even when you aren't a parent. You can see the joy in people's eyes when they are with their children, or the heartache with which they talk about them when they are separated.

Sure, it is hard, but there is a reason why people do it again and again and again. Because the love is limitless.

Would I do it again? I get asked this all the time and my truthful answer is that the only thing stopping me is finances. I have worked every day since I graduated, I have been gifted money from dead parents and yet still I have had to sell my home to be able to sleep without the crippling worry of how I am going to pay for childcare or to clear the monthly credit card bill. (Again, I can't reiterate enough that this is also because I am shit with money and I insist on sending people presents all the time to show them I love them when it is wildly unnecessary, so it is not all Herb!)

So, if I could take the harsh practicalities of money out of it – of paying for the privilege or finding someone who could share the mortgage and the childcare costs with me – would I do it again? In a heartbeat. If I fell in love tomorrow and I could become pregnant with them and, even better, that someone could bring a couple of willing grandparents into the fold, then absolutely I would have as many as my body and kitchen table would allow. With all that said, though, I am so wildly happy with my boy that who am I to try to rock our beautifully stable, healthy boat? Herbert

Leonard Elvis is a total rock star. He is healthy, happy, passionate, curious, wild and loved. I don't have the right to try to ask for that again, to demand more of the same. While I do crave it, it would feel like some incredible kind of greed. I haven't suffered maternal loss, I haven't had soul-destroying test results given to me by doctors, I haven't had to make him endure any real hardships, I haven't had to share him with anyone. We are so privileged, I feel that I have hit the jackpot, and you rarely win the lottery twice, do you?

I also feel that we are at a time when we can truly create the life we want. The fetters of a more rigid family dynamic are slowly coming loose. That is not to say that I don't think a family with a mum and a dad and lots of siblings isn't wonderful. How could I? That is how I was raised. What I do strongly believe, though, is that there are people longing to carve out their own magnificent family adventure who, for an abundance of reasons, don't fit into the narrative that for so long we have been informed is 'normal'. So, is that to say that they shouldn't try to clasp on to their dreams? Fuck no. I think it means they can dig deep, grab their fantasies by the horns and wave them round for all to see. To rejoice in the knowledge that there are other paths out there. They may not be the well-trodden ones, but that is OK, you can cut down the overgrown brambles and bloody stamp through to create a path to your very own idea of heaven. Some will do it alone and some will have their hands held throughout. What I am saying is it doesn't matter how it happens; if we want it, we have to do everything we can to try to capture it.

Of course, just sheer will and determination doesn't always make for a happy ending. Life is too often rife with tragedy and upset, with disappointments beyond our wildest hopes. Yet for me, who is pretty au fait with this, having had my fair share of shit hitting the fan, I just couldn't sit back and wait for my time to pass me by, no matter what setbacks I might have encountered in the process. And so here I am, nearly five years after making that momentous decision to go it alone, and I couldn't be happier that I decided to join the ride.

I am totally, absolutely, truly and wholeheartedly thrilled with how our little team is turning out, in spite of any hurdles we are having to jump – whether 'normal' or totally unanticipated ones like a global pandemic! Herb wouldn't get into the bath for nearly a year due to a sudden inexplicable fear of all water except puddles; I am pretty certain he has eaten horse shit; I don't pole-vault over to him at the meekest sound of a cry; I used to let him crawl around super-markets freely because it gave him such deep joy. He has never once tried to get out of his cot, so he is still in one, and so far, he hasn't ever vaguely given a notion that he is up for being potty trained so he is still sadly adding to the nappy landfill. I swear in front of him, he watches more TV than I would like, he can't drink out of a cup without it spilling everywhere, he will often hug a worm so tight they may not live another minute, he would happily only eat gherkins, fish fingers and crisps, he tells me off when I sing, he makes his teddies smell his stinky nappy and we fight about his bloody dummy almost hourly. However, he is so happy and loved, and as long as he isn't in sixth form college in a nappy, with a dummy and bottle of milk, then all these things can wait. I am in no rush.

For all his brilliantly feral nature that is to be expected from a toddler finding his way, he brings about such unbridled joy. He belly laughs when you gurn at him, he eats spaghetti like it is the world's most exciting toy, his eyes absolutely sparkle when he sees our family, his grin can literally light up a room. Strangers in parks seek me out to compliment me on what a lovely polite boy he is, his laugh is guttural and infectious, he is inherently polite, he can say

Pachycephalosaurus perfectly but calls mushrooms 'lushrooms'. He is absolutely enchanted by animals and his deepest joy is when he is outside in a wood, jumping in puddles, kicking leaves, collecting sticks and searching for owls. He is pure joy.

I cannot believe I made him on my own, with just a touch of science and the kindness of a man I am unlikely to ever meet. I am beyond grateful to Herb, every single day – he has allowed me to know how very deeply my battered, bruised and tired heart can love. I have already started to talk to Herb openly and truthfully about how we became a family. I have no intention of hiding him away from any of it, for him to ever feel anything other than the fact he was so intensely longed for that I decided to do everything in my power to make him a reality, to create our very own tribe.

This story of how he came to be and how we thrived in our first few years together may well be drawing to a close, but our little family adventure is only just starting – and I am so bloody excited about what is to come. Buckle up, kid. Let's go!

DEAR DONOR . . .[1]

I don't even know where to start, but I owe it to you to try:

We have never met, but you gave me the world.

I don't know your name, but I carried your genes.

I wouldn't recognise your face, but you changed my life.

You gave me the chance to live my dreams, but I don't know yours.

Together we've created a life, but I've never even heard you laugh.

You allowed me to know unconditional love, but who holds your heart?

My maternal instinct was born via you, but I don't know if you are a dad.

---

1 This is taken from an Instagram post I was asked to write in conjunction with Giovanna Fletcher's *Letters on Motherhood* in February 2020

My world revolves around half your genetics, but what makes you feel whole?

As you enjoy your daily life, in another country, chatting in another language, I need you to know that my world is complete because of you. I hope you are as happy as you have allowed me to be. I think you are extraordinary. Every time my son holds my hand, I thank you. Whenever he looks up at me, I wonder if he has your eyes. When he is stubborn, I blame you!

You gave me the most amazing gift and I promise you, I will do everything in my power to ensure my son grows up happy, immersed in love and knowing he can make his dreams come true. Just like his mum did, because of you.

Thank you, dear donor, thank you.

Liv

x

HERB, MY DARLING
BOY . . .

I hope you don't mind that I shared our story. You see, I am so utterly proud of you, of me, of our little family, and I want to scream it from the rooftops, to show everyone that they can also make their dreams come true. I wished for you so strongly, I hoped for you so ferociously that sometimes I still cannot believe that I made you, all by myself. That every glorious part of you was born from me.

I want you to know that you too have the ability to create your own path, wherever you want it to lead. My dearest wish is for you to know every day how very, utterly loved you are. I yearn for your life to be one of compassion, of tenderness, of wonder, of happiness and a real sense of humanity. My hope is for you to love as deeply as you are loved. For my loss to be replaced by your joy. Your hopes to be limitless. Your health to be infinite.

You healed parts of me I didn't know were broken and you opened up my heart for me to proudly put it out into the world. You are funny, kind, charming and generous and my pride in you is unrivalled. I know the days that you need me to guide you, hold your hand and nurture you will be all too fleeting, so I will remember to celebrate your magic, always. I will forever encourage all your passions and will always be your number one cheerleader, because you my boy, are 'the only thing in this whole world that is pure and good and right,' as the great philosopher Meat Loaf once declared! You see, I will always be here to embarrass you, too, and that is never going to change. Sorry, kid. Just know that it all comes from a place of authentic devotion to you and your happiness and that you have made me feel entirely whole. Thank you.

I love you, Herbalicious. Never change.

Mum

x

ACKNOWLEDGMENTS

I am not officially a writer, but I do have a story to tell. Being given the opportunity to write this book has been a wild privilege. One that absolutely would not have been possible with a two-year-old, three house moves and a full-time job during a pandemic, had it not been for my amazing friends and family. Any whiff of easing of lockdowns and they would be over in a flash to look after Herb so I could have time to put my words down. I am forever grateful. Obviously this should all be read in the style of Gwynnie P's infamous Oscar speech.

Belly . . . where do I start? I can hand on heart say that without you I don't think I would have made it through the last four years. The way you have loved and nurtured Herb has been amazing to witness. He adores you and is so lucky to have you, but not as lucky as me. Thank you. (Yeah, yeah, I will do some yoga.)

Silly . . . I can't tell you how grateful I am for all your M4 trips over the last three years. For the middle-of-the-night calls, for you holding me when I was falling apart. Thank you with my whole heart for letting us stay 'for a while' (four months and counting!) and teaching Herb about the joys of figs and peanut butter. He loves them nearly as much as he loves you. Me too.

Miguel . . . Thank you for always believing in me and cheering me on. Thank you for always helping out when I need it most. Don't worry, your time for sleepovers will come now that he is walking and talking . . . you need to teach him how to race cars, just not motorbikes, OK? I know I am secretly your favourite . . .

The Rainbows . . . you have welcomed Herb into your life with such massive open arms that I am pretty sure he loves you guys more than me. Arch, Evie, Es . . . thank you, thank you for letting him take over your rooms on sleepovers, for baking with him, for reading to him, for teaching him guitar, for basically keeping him alive for the last three years. I promise to pay it forward when the time comes. And Rain, thank you for your patience and opening your home to my boy, just like you did for me all those years ago.

The Niecephews . . . Molly, Finn, Kitt, Hebe, Pip, Holly Dolly, Jim Jam, Arch, Evie Weevs and Bezzie Boo . . .

All of you have given me so much strength over the last few years. You are the ones who showed me how to love limitlessly. Herb is obsessed with all of you and he is so bloody lucky to have you. Thank you all for helping out as much as you have, I honestly cannot tell you how much it has meant to me for you to give me your time and Herb your love. An especially big bear hug to Kitty, for looking after Herb so much on our 'brief' sojourn to Devon . . . you were legendary. I look forward to each of you dressing up as the Easter Bunny in years to come, or Father Christmas. Your choice . . .

CCA . . . You agreeing to come and support me and freely giving up your time to me when I needed you the most was bloody wonderful. Thank you for not showing anyone the photos of me in labour! Sorry I made you witness that. Thank you most of all for giving me that gentle push that summer, without that, Herb may not be mine.

Team Godparent . . . He has only been around for three years, but already you have shown him such a whacking great big dose of love and kindness that you may have spoilt him for life. Thank you for agreeing to be such a huge part of Herb's life, he is going to need each and every one of you if he is going to survive living with just me!

Leila . . . because I didn't actually name a chapter after you. Soz, bumface.

Team Herd . . . thank you for never questioning my commitment to our brilliant business. Without your trust and support I would never have been able to do this. I am forever grateful and can't wait to see how many houses the next four years can bring.

Toddy and SBB . . . Thank you for everything, for being so patient and kind with Herb and for tolerating me and all my endless phone calls to your other halves!

Alison and Lisa . . . the best childminders in all the land. Herb is so bloomin' #blessed to have had you and your families show him so much love and care and mud.

Everyone . . . who has shown Herb and I such unconditional love, support and kindness over the last few years . . . Auntie Ann and Anton, Dee and Arthur, Mumma Rosa, Richie, Jim, Jane and Terry, Hilly and Alan, Auntie Di and Tim, Amy M, The Wonderful Websters, Lovely Kate, Kelly Dawn, Kryton (never Dan!) and Jenny Spen, all my amazing godsprogs, The Girls, Lynney, Cafff, Em Ten, TFunk, Sal, Jane M, Jean, Tim F, Phoebe Rainbird and everyone on Port Meadow who cheered me on and hugged me when I cried. Thank you.

Briony, Lauren and Grace . . . thank you for your faith in me, for always putting my sanity above any deadlines and for allowing the cover to not have pastel-coloured baby bottles!

Team Instagram . . . Lorna, Charlotte, Liv, Kelly, Cora, Anna, Vickie, Alice, Holly, Steph, Baxter, Anna, Elle, Jess, Dom, Laura, Cam, Clemmie T, Shivlet, Nicola, Bex, Louise, Grace, Suse, Clover, Emma, Paige, Ellie, Bab, Nic, Tanya, George, Michelle, Nikki, Kaytee, Cat, Petra, Erin, Ro, Jem, Giovanna, Erin, Elly, Sara, Nicki, Gem, Beth, Ele, Mia, Kerry, Alex, Cat, Illy, Nicola, Rachel, Claire and Sarah – I mean, there are hundreds of you, literally, and I know I will have forgotten someone – but the support and beautiful friendships those little squares have given me when I have been having wobbles in the middle of the night has been a lifeline. Thank you from the bottom of my tired heart!

Elvis . . . when everyone else had someone, I had you. You saved me. You are never allowed to go. Deal? There is a sausage in it for you.

Jen . . . Party on, my Bubble. I miss you every day.

Mum and Dad . . . Forever my inspiration. You'd both adore him. I hope we make you proud. I had a go.

An invitation from the publisher

Join us at www.hodder.co.uk, or follow us
on Twitter @hodderbooks to be a part of
our community of people who love the very
best in books and reading.

Whether you want to discover more about a book
or an author, watch trailers and interviews, have the
chance to win early limited editions, or simply browse
our expert readers' selection of the very best books,
we think you'll find what you're looking for.

And if you don't, that's the place to tell us what's missing.

We love what we do, and we'd love you to be a part of it.

www.hodder.co.uk

 @hodderbooks

HodderBooks

 HodderBooks